R. Dandridge Collins has brought, in
and a tender heart to those in need o
ing. This significant and insightful u
wounded accept the marvelous grace o
ability and the will to move on.

> Rev. J. Wendell Mapson, Jr.
> President, Baptist Ministers
> Philadelphia Conference and Vicinity
> Pastor, Monumental Baptist Church,
> Philadelphia, PA

Dr. Collins has produced a work that will bless the lives of believers for years to come. Many Christians walk around trapped in The Trauma Zone *not knowing that there are exits signs in that "zone" to point the believer to the doors through which a follower of Christ may walk with confidence and with a cure for the disease with which they have been living for so long!*

Dr. Collins' Trauma D.J. keeps many persons of faith listening to a constant negative "rap" and also keeps them living beneath their dignity. They live with brokenness and unhealed wounds. Dr. Collins shows in the pages of this work how Christ will heal those wounds and how, when we walk along with Christ, we can become whole again.

I recommend his book to all who are in the helping professions. I recommend his book to all who wrestle with depression and negative attitudes. I recommend his book to all who would embrace what it is that Jesus had in His mind when He said, "I have come that you might have life more abundantly!"

> Pastor Jeremiah A. Wright
> Trinity United Church of Christ
> Chicago, IL

I am pleased to add my hearty endorsement to this well-written, insightful, and helpful treatment of a subject near and dear to my heart and absolutely essential to an effective holistic pastoral ministry. In some very important ways it is a timely, long awaited practical resource for every pastor's and counselor's reading that effectively combines biblical and theological and spiritual discernment with documented clinical research. It is a must read for all ministers concerned about helping people to achieve what Jesus meant when He said, "Be thou made whole!"

> Rev. Dr. Albert F. Campbell
> Pastor, Mount Carmel Baptist Church
> Philadelphia, PA

The Trauma Zone *is a well-written, user-friendly guide that will empower the reader to navigate the often tortuous path toward healing. By using real world examples, Dr. Collins affirms that there is hope for those who feel trapped in the trauma zone and highlights the pathways out of it. I will recommend this book to my patients who struggle with trauma and its aftereffects.*

Tracey Jones, M.D.
Board Eligible Child Psychiatrist

Reading The Trauma Zone: Trusting God for Emotional Healing *is both rewarding and enlightening. R. Dandridge Collins has provided a usable and helpful book in practical readable style that delves into some of the toughest areas of in-depth psychotherapy. It is a must read for pastors, counselors, and individuals trying to get a deeper understanding of the traumas that hamper people from finding true joy and peace in life.*

Wallace Charles Smith, President
The Palmer Theological Seminary of Eastern University
Wynnewood, PA

In The Trauma Zone: Trusting God for Emotional Healing, *Dr. Collins brilliantly presents strategies that reflect his training in both the psychological and religious arenas. Dr. Collins' down-to-earth approach and his unique integration of psychological principles and biblical insights make this book useful to survivors, their families and friends, and the professionals who treat/interact with them. Of particular interest are the chapters dealing with the "Three-Headed Monsters: flashbacks, nightmares and intrusive thoughts." I highly recommend this work to everyone relating to Christian survivors of trauma.*

Melvin Rogers, Ph.D.
Clinical Psychologist
Past President
Pennsylvania Psychological Association

the**TRAUMA**zone

TRUSTING GOD FOR EMOTIONAL HEALING

R. DANDRIDGE COLLINS, PH.D.

MOODY PUBLISHERS

CHICAGO

The Trauma Zone is a self-help guide for people who have endured significant emotional pain. The ideas in this book are not intended to substitute for professional support when it is needed. If the issue of self-harm arises, professional help is urged.

Identifying information was altered to protect the anonymity of the people who shared their stories. Some accounts are not stories of single individuals *(chapters 6, 8, 16, 17, and 22)*, but are compilations of the stories of many clients.

Scripture quotations marked NLT are taken from the *Holy Bible, New Living Translation,* copyright © 1996, 2004. Used by permission of Tyndale House Publishers, Inc., Wheaton Illinois 60189, U.S.A. All rights reserved.

Editor: Francesca Gray
Cover Design: David Holman
Image Credit: Getty Images and Innate Perceptions, Inc.
Interior Design: Ragont Designs

Library of Congress Cataloging-in-Publication Data

Collins, R. Dandridge.
    The trauma zone / by R. Dandridge Collins.
        p. cm.
    Includes bibliographical references.
    ISBN-13: 978-0-8024-8989-0
    ISBN-10: 0-8024-8989-3
    1. Post-traumatic stress disorder—Patients—Religious life. 2. Post-traumatic stress disorder—Religious aspects—Christianity. 3. Psychic trauma—Religious aspects—Christianity. 4. Spiritual healing. 5. Psychology, Religious. 6. Mental health—Religious aspects—Christianity. I. Title.

BV4910.45.C65 2006
248.8'6--dc22

2006028787

1 3 5 7 9 10 8 6 4 2

Printed in the United States of America

*This book is dedicated
to the wonderful people I serve
whose journey out of The Trauma Zone
mandated that I chronicle their progress
so others could be helped.
I also dedicate this labor of love
to my wife, Delores Foster Collins,
whose steadfast support means more to me
than she will ever know.*

Contents

Foreword

The Trauma Zone: Trusting God for Emotional Healing is a must have for every pastor's library. Dr. Collins has gamely woven together in the fabric of his book solid clinical insight with profound biblical understanding. His down-to-earth writing style takes the complicated issue of emotional trauma and organizes it in a way that even a child can understand it. And I say this as a high compliment of the author's ability to interpret the intricacies of psychological and spiritual suffering, and relate it back to us in a way that is strikingly clear.

The Trauma Zone is an important resource for the church. Broken relationships and tattered dreams have thrown many people into the darkness of their own despair. In the shadows of our personal anguish, we grope for the light but often come up empty-handed. In this book, Dr. Collins' words serve as a personal guide that walks you through and prays you through each aspect of trauma.

The cornerstone of what *The Trauma Zone* teaches us is that when we understand how trauma works, we learn a truth that has uncanny power, that there are exit signs to our pain, that our misery has an end if we just know how to access the help we need. Dr. Collins shows us the way out of our pain, in his masterful style of interpreting the Scripture and use of psychological insight.

The practical language he employs makes *The Trauma Zone* a user-friendly document for lay people. The problem of emotional trauma, however, is so widespread that it is also invaluable to Christian professionals of many disciplines who see people suffering, and want to offer them a resource that can usher them into the light.

So who could benefit from reading *The Trauma Zone*? Survivors of abuse and neglect, wartime veterans, terrorists' attacks, etc.

When we have been down and out, we need hope. *The Trauma Zone* offers Christians a powerful tool that helps us see that beyond our pain we can finally embrace a more complete vibrant life. This book exemplifies what our Saviour meant when He said, "I am come that ye may have life and that ye may have it more abundantly" (John 10:10).

Dr. William J. Shaw
President, National Baptist Convention, USA, Inc.
Pastor, White Rock Baptist Church
Philadelphia, PA

Acknowledgments

SINCE I BEGAN THE WORK of documenting the meaningful improvement that my clients were making from their trauma, no one has been more inspirational and available than Marlene Bagnull, LittD. Her creative editing has strengthened the message in this manuscript. I also am grateful to my wife, Delores, who spent countless hours editing the manuscript, staying up with me, and sacrificing many opportunities to get a good night's sleep. Cynthia Ballenger, of Moody Publishers Lift Every Voice imprint, has been invaluable in her support, genuine kindness, and resourcefulness.

I appreciate my mother, Mary Ruth Collins, whose prayerful support is a sustaining force in my life. I also want to recognize the encouragement of my three adult children, Harold; Terry and his wife, Jessica; and Darielle. I appreciate my children taking literally the biblical command to "be fruitful and multiply" because they have blessed me with seven beautiful grandchildren: Angela, Christopher, Breanna, Jeremiah, Caleb, Michael, and Daniel.

I also acknowledge fellow pastoral counselors, Randolph

Walters, PsyD, and Vincent Calloway, MSS, LSW, for their friendship and selfless nurturance of my ideas of transforming trauma. My hat goes off to A. Njideka Brown, MA, MS, for her belief in the effectiveness of *The Trauma Zone* model during its formative stages. I also want to express appreciation to Minister Debbie Combs, MDiv, for her helpful research support as this project got underway.

I am grateful to my pastor, Rev. Dr. J. Wendell Mapson Jr., and the Monumental Baptist Church for being a true church family. I am also thankful for the ministers who honor me by sending their members to our practice, the Pastoral Counseling Network, for additional support.

I appreciate John Brendler, Chris Simms, and my gifted colleagues at Building Bridges in Media, PA, for creating such an excellent practice environment. I am indebted to the caring professionals at my office in Philadelphia who consistently go out of their way to be helpful. Thanks to Dominic D'Ortenzio, whose hospitality with my clients makes an office visit seem like a homecoming.

My heartfelt appreciation for the nurturing and support that I received from my colleagues in ministry at Palmer Theological Seminary in Philadelphia, where I was trained and have served for the past four decades.

Thanks to Deborah K. Witt, MD, for trusting me with so many of her clients over the years. I extend special thanks to my good friends Chris Coxe, Irving Perkins, and Rev. James Pickens, who went the extra mile in helping me complete this manuscript. Thanks to everyone I call friend; you were with me as I wrote.

Introduction

I GREW UP IN A TIME of television innocence.
Some of the landmark TV shows of this era were *Leave It to
Beaver, Julia, Ozzie and Harriet, The Andy Griffith Show,*
and, of course, *Batman.* Juxtaposed against this backdrop of
wholesomeness and comfort was *The Twilight Zone,* which
for me, in elementary school, was a disquieting and spooky
show. In *The Twilight Zone,* some hapless victim always
stumbled into some kind of misadventure and ended up
trapped in a stressful situation. Nothing ever fully made
sense in *The Twilight Zone.* The rules of time and space were
suspended. But this much was clear: if you were unfortunate
enough to find yourself in *The Twilight Zone,* nothing was
more important than getting out.

The Bible is filled with examples of people who found themselves in a difficult situation and needed to escape. I am convinced that the Hebrew people who left the oppression of Egypt
understood how nerve-racking it is to be in a "twilight zone"
experience. It's a space they were familiar with, between oppression and deliverance, promise and fulfillment. The Hebrew
people were in limbo. They were in search of a land flowing

with "milk and honey," but they got stuck instead in a menacing wilderness on the journey from Egypt to Canaan (see Numbers 13:1–14:24).

The same is true for the people I serve today as a therapist at the Pastoral Counseling Network in Philadelphia. Many are posttraumatic stress survivors. Most, like brave soldiers, carried on with their lives until new demands brought the old wounds storming back to the surface. These courageous souls all seem to be in a zone, a strange *trauma zone*. And like *The Twilight Zone*, many things just don't make sense. In this trauma zone, the usual rules of living a comfortable and sane life have been suspended.

Trauma zone dwellers have an existence that is full of "can'ts." These can'ts form an organized network, like distinct stops—stations—on a train route.

1. **Can't Cope with Your Emotions.** The very nature of trauma is to become overwhelmed with your emotions. Your feelings become too hot to handle. Somehow, by God's grace, you survive; but you notice something is different about you now. You are inundated by your feelings. Sometimes you feel your emotions so intensely that it hurts to feel. It's easier at times to feel nothing at all.

   On the other end of the spectrum, your reactions may become so forceful that they feel unmanageable: sadness becomes depression, anger becomes rage, and anxiety turns into panic. The classic patterns of "fight or flight" slide into operation here too. And because it seems as if you can't cope with your feelings, a domino effect is created in other areas. Your fears may immobilize you. Your pain may torment you to such a degree that you live in the past. Reality may hurt so much that you may choose to live in a world of fantasy or denial, or even worse to get hooked on anything that will deaden the pain. All of the other trauma stations are a by-product of this one.

2. Can't Tell Time. In this station of *The Trauma Zone,* you are so besieged by pain from the past that you become distracted from living your life in the present. Nightmares, flashbacks, and intrusive thoughts all play a part in keeping you at this station and from becoming grounded in the here and now. It is commonplace to get the past confused with the present. Something that may have happened years ago seems as though it is happening right now.

3. Can't Move. I have noticed that trauma survivors at this station often complain of feeling stuck. You share how hard it is to move on and leave behind disturbing memories and bad experiences. In this station, you often feel like a victim and do not know how to get out of this position. You describe yourself as being frozen, like a deer caught in the headlights of an automobile. The mere process of making a decision becomes painful in this trauma station. You procrastinate. Your self-esteem is gone. And you have an overall lack of life progress.

4. Can't Learn. People in this station keep repeating the same mistakes. You may find yourself engaging in addictive behaviors (alcohol abuse, crack use, sex, romance, work, shopping, etc.), often in the face of mounting evidence that the practice is not working. The expression, "Insanity is doing the same thing over and over again and expecting a different result," applies here. Relationship failure is also prominent. Unfortunately, because you have undergone extreme stress you have a tendency to change partners without changing yourself.

When this happens, you blame others for your mistakes. Invariably, you don't learn from your pain. A pattern of relationship failure, both personal and professional, comes cascading down on you.

5. **Can't See.** Survivors at this station are in a state of denial, like an ostrich with its head buried in the sand. You handle your pain in lots of creative ways. You pretend your pain does not exist. You act as though what you have been through is no big deal. You block difficult memories from your mind.

These five stations form the boundaries of *The Trauma Zone*. Like the people in the fictional *Twilight Zone*, the survivors in the real-life trauma zone have, as their most important need, the need to find a way out. When people understand how trauma works and how to get loosed from its tenacious grip, they are set free to live their lives unencumbered by the wounds of the past. That's the good news I've discovered in working with hundreds of people. There is hope! They have found—and you can too—that there is a way out.

The words of the psalmist ring true to provide extra courage and inspiration to God's children who are in *The Trauma Zone*. Hear the psalmist:

Even if my father and mother abandon me, the Lord will hold me close. Teach me how to live, O Lord. Lead me along the right path, for my enemies are waiting for me. Do not let me fall into their hands. For they accuse me of things I've never done; with every breath they threaten me with violence. Yet I am confident I will see the Lord's goodness while I am here in the land of the living. Wait patiently

for the Lord. Be brave and courageous.
Yes, wait patiently for the Lord.

—Psalm 27:10–14

The psalmist helps us to understand that although testing and hardship are often unwelcome visitors on our journey, we are not alone. God is with us to protect, guide, and comfort us. This is crucial for us to know. Trauma is something that should never be faced alone. We need God's help to lead us through the storm and take us to "higher ground." In practical terms, higher ground may well be asking for human support.

When exiting *The Trauma Zone,* select a support person (see Appendix C) to help with your healing journey. It is important that you choose someone with whom you feel very comfortable sharing intimate details of your life. The person needs to be available, reliable, mature, and dedicated to keeping what you share confidential. If the person you are thinking of has been consistently available for you, explore if he or she can be a confidant as you commit to working through your trauma.

As you prayerfully reflect on whom you will ask to walk with you through this journey, it will also be important that your support person is able to handle the range of emotions you may encounter. If dealing with emotionally charged information sets him or her off, you might want to consider someone else you feel can handle your emotions. Remember that the person you ask to support you is your choice. Don't choose someone out of a sense of obligation. Instead, choose someone who is a good match for your healing journey.

Your support person can be a professional such as your minister or counselor. Your support person can also be a layperson, family member, or friend—someone who is empathetic and consistently available to commit time and emotional energy to your healing. If you feel you don't have a family member or friend you can turn to for support, then ask your physician for a referral to a counseling center or a behavioral health professional. You can also check the blue pages of your phone book.

Emotional trauma is tricky and powerful. Just when you think you have loosed yourself from its grip, trauma pulls you back and laughs in your face. Despite the setbacks, do not despair. God's ability to heal is stronger than trauma's ability to wound. Part One unfolds the battle plan for finding the hope you need to begin your healing journey. Let's walk together.

Preparing for the Battle

Emotional trauma has the capacity to spin you in circles. You need lots of support, and one of the sources you need support from is yourself. In particular, trauma sets off a voice in your soul—a tape that is filled with negative thoughts. When you heed the messages from this negative tape, you remain stuck in The Trauma Zone. I call the inner voice of your emotional pain the "Trauma DJ." In the first chapter let's look at how the Trauma DJ operates so we can identify how to transform the Trauma DJ into a calming inner voice that speaks peace to your soul.

chapter 1

The Trauma **DJ**

TRAUMA IS LIFE'S ULTIMATE TEST. It pushes you to the edge of your breaking point. Each of us, at some time, faces a life circumstance that is so trying that we feel like crumbling. It could be the death of a loved one. Or it could be something else: divorce, incest, infidelity, sudden job loss, church blowups . . . All can be crucibles that leave us reeling in emotional pain for years. The aftermath of this trauma is for the survivors to be left with a strange, uncomfortable voice, like a tape playing in their heads. It's the voice of the Trauma DJ.

Sometimes the voice of the Trauma DJ thunders. Sometimes the voice whispers. Usually it's a nonstop chatterbox that speaks to you, keeping you on edge. The Trauma DJ speaks to your heart, leaving you stymied, frozen, and overwhelmed. You feel like hiding and taking cover. You end up feeling like a chicken running in circles with its head cut off. You feel trapped in a time warp that is embedded in your past as you relive your nightmares a thousand times.

For some people, the Trauma DJ assumes the form of a

disturbing image. It can be a flashback—a snapshot of a tragic experience that litters the landscape of your mind.

Tricky and tenacious, trauma slips on the noose and tries to strangle you. The Trauma DJ whips your feelings into a frenzy by getting you to buy into the thinking that your life can never change. It's a kind of "once bruised always damaged" type of thinking.

The Trauma DJ counsels you to expect the worst from life and people. It points to your life experiences that have been tragically painful. It convinces you (to prevent an encore performance of pain) to be on guard. Be ready to duck. And if necessary, duke it out. "Don't take no stuff!"

The voice of the Trauma DJ is persistent and overbearing. When you heed its advice, it binds you up, like a ball and chain.

The Trauma DJ has a message with your name on it. Based on your personal crucible, the internal tape begins to play, saying:

- *"What's the point in even trying? You'll never . . ."*

- *"They never supported you before. What makes you think it will be different now?"*

- *"Remember when things fell apart before? You might as well not even bother now."*

And the beat goes on. The voice of the Trauma DJ is persistent and overbearing. When you heed its advice, it binds you up, like a ball and chain. When you follow its instructions, it renders you powerless.

That's the bad news. The good news is that the Trauma DJ is akin to a broken fire alarm system. It goes off daily when there is neither fire nor danger. The work of healing from your emotional pain is to identify when the Trauma DJ is sending out another false alarm and to tune it out. The challenge is to learn how to relax and calmly face whatever the Lord allows. Trauma tends to make you an emotional basket case if you let it. So remember that the Trauma DJ always speaks in the language of exaggeration.

Allow your mistakes to be your mentors.

When the Trauma DJ overwhelms you with a recurring problem, one that has tripped you up many times before, slow it down a bit. Take it easy and learn from your errors. Allow your mistakes to be your mentors. When the Trauma DJ tries to persuade you that past tragedies will hunt you down and haunt you forever, say "hogwash." Say to yourself, "Then was then and now is now." Remind yourself that you can choose to live powerfully in the present.

When the Trauma DJ tries to paralyze you with fear to the point that you feel you can't move, just keep walking, one step at a time, and you'll march out of *The Trauma Zone.* When the Trauma DJ whips your emotions into a frenzy and you are inclined to overreact with sadness, anger, or fear, just remember that the Trauma DJ's message is overstated. Stay calm and respond to your challenges with the strength that comes from God's love.

The Trauma DJ is a fearmonger. But remember the words of Paul to the church at Corinth. God never tests us past our breaking point. Instead, His tests are designed for our good. They are intended to bring out Christian character.

The temptations in your life are no different from what others experience. And God is faithful. He will not allow the temptation to be more than you can stand. When you are tempted, he will show you a way out so that you can endure.

—1 Corinthians 10:13

God is able to transform our emotional hurts into spiritual gain by making us more discerning, wise, and loving of self and others. This newfound understanding helps us to sort out both external and internal distractions. The Trauma DJ is an internal distraction. Its message of doom and gloom is never fully accurate. Instead, it is the voice of cover-up.

We can choose to listen to another voice—the voice of recovery. This voice of the Holy Spirit calms us, renews us, and redirects us. This voice encourages and inspires. This voice connects with hope and an uplifting vision that leads us out of *The Trauma Zone* and into a relationship with the Good Shepherd. "My sheep listen to my voice," Jesus said. "I know them, and they follow me" (John 10:27).

ACTION STEPS

1. **Learn to quickly recognize the Trauma DJ based on the negative messages that it gives you about yourself in particular or life in general.** Sometimes the message is a put-down of who you are or your abilities. Sometimes the message creates a pessimistic view of others. If you buy into these negative messages, they will keep you stuck in *The Trauma Zone.*

2. **Pray for wisdom to quiet the voice of the Trauma DJ in your life.** God's wisdom will help you discern healthy

self-reflection from toxic negative thinking. Healthy self-reflection enables you to look objectively at how you can improve and grow. The thinking generated by the Trauma DJ never helps because it only makes you more indecisive and afraid to live your life to the fullest as God intended.

3. **Study God's Word.** Fill your mind with God's promises that represent His ideas about you and the wonderful plan He has for you. Meditation is one excellent way to fill your mind with God's promises. Choose some of your favorite Scriptures. The book of Psalms is a great place to start when you are going through a difficult time. Allow your mind to think about God's Word and how it applies to your life today. Meditating on God's promises creates enormous life-giving spiritual energy. You will find that what you think about makes all the difference in the world. Remember His promise:

You will keep in perfect peace all who trust in you, all whose thoughts are fixed on you!—Isaiah 26:3

Let's Pray Together

Father, many of us have been through the wringer emotionally. We learned to listen to a voice that was not Yours. It was the voice of our pain, our fear, and our doubt. It was the voice of the Trauma DJ. Teach us today to override the voice of our misery with the voice of Your mercy. Help us to overcome the voice of fear with the voice of faith. Empower us to conquer the voice of defeat with the voice of Your overwhelming, life-transforming love. Remind us, dear Father, that there is a way out of our heartache and that You will show us the way. Amen.

TOGETHER LET'S BEGIN TO
PLOT THE ROAD MAP FOR EXITING
YOUR PERSONAL TRAUMA ZONE.

chapter 2

The Trauma ZONE
Has Exit Signs

REMEMBERING A TRAGIC EXPERIENCE is gut-wrenching! One of the first things I do when working with people who have experienced something traumatic is to give them hope before we begin to take on the monsters in *The Trauma Zone*.

I encourage them to think of *The Trauma Zone* as a landmark that they can use to let them know that they have gone too far. Understanding the trauma landmark enables them to recognize that they are in an unfamiliar neighborhood. The remedy comes from slowing down, making a safe U-turn, and heading in the right direction.

I have an exit sign in the waiting room of my office. Often, at the end of the first session, I point to the sign and say, "*The Trauma Zone* has exit signs." I usually get a big smile and a nod of the head. The message has gotten through. Their pain can heal. Their trauma doesn't have the last word. They have the last word. You do too! You can make choices, one step at a time, to reverse the effects of your pain.

One of those steps is to make a U-turn. In the process of

healing, a U-turn can be an act of transformation. When you are beset by your burdens, it is easy to fall into a victim mode. But when you stand up to your trauma, you begin your road to recovery.

Overwhelming stress does strange things to you. One of the biggest changes that overtakes you is that trauma saps your power. It makes you feel helpless and fearful.

We all know what it is like to be a child and afraid of the dark. The experience of being stuck in the midst of your own personal trauma is akin to being a child in a very dark room groping for the light switch. Darkness and fear are "roommates." Breaking free from the grip of trauma is all about learning how to face and manage your fears.

The Holy Spirit equips the believer with the power to get things done and to be effective.

Second Timothy 1:7 is a wonderful building block to help you corral the spirit of fear. Listen to Paul's words: "For God has not given us a spirit of fear and timidity, but of power, love, and self-discipline."

Meditate on this Scripture. Let its words soak into the soil of your soul. The spirit of trauma causes you to live in fear. This kind of stress makes your soul quake. But when you meditate on the three principles in this passage, you realize that God does not want you to be intimidated. Instead, the Holy Spirit equips the believer with the *power* to get things done and to be effective. He gives us *love* that keeps us nurtured and protected. And He gives us *self-discipline* that keeps us focused in the right direction and grounded in hope. When you put these three together—*power, love,* and *self-discipline*—they become a wonderful spiritual fortress protecting you from evil yet at the same time giving you the tools to face it.

Healing comes from taking your power back. Defying trauma and the voice of the Trauma DJ is a first step in reclaiming your power.

One of the best role models for reclaiming power comes from the pages of African-American history in the person of Frederick Douglass. He was an eloquent critic of the institution of slavery. Masters knew that the only way they could keep people enslaved was by "getting into their heads" and instilling fear. Flogging was a way they sought to intimidate their slaves. One day, when Frederick was only sixteen, his master took him to a flogger who beat him unmercifully. Frederick remained "defiant," and his master later sent him back for another flogging. The result this time was very different. Frederick fought him back! And from his ordeal with the flogger he penned these memorable sayings:

Defying trauma and the voice of the Trauma DJ is a first step in reclaiming your power.

Power only backs up in the face of raw power.
Power concedes nothing without a demand.

What this means for the survivor is that trauma must be defied. I tell my counselees to do the opposite of what the Trauma DJ tells them to do. I ask them to identify the trauma station they feel they are in, and then I remind them that *The Trauma Zone Has Exit Signs!*

ACTION STEPS ⬇

1. **Are there times when you have felt helpless?** Remember that you are *not* helpless nor are you a victim.

2. **Specify *one* thing you can do to reclaim your power.**

3. **Consider how love can make a difference.**

4. **Identify an area of your life where you need to exercise more self-discipline.**

5. **Note one thing the Trauma DJ is telling you to do, and choose to do the opposite.**

Let's Pray Together

Lord, give me the strength to face my fears. I know sometimes life can be scary. People do cruel things to each other. Some people use their words like sledgehammers. But that's their problem. I have found new strength because You are greater than my trouble. You are my healer.

Help me today to step out from under the shadow of fear and to live victoriously. I am not a victim. I am not helpless. "For I can do everything through Christ, who gives me strength" (Philippians 4:13). With You by my side I can face the storm that rages inside of me. Help me today to reclaim my power. Thank You, Lord, for hearing my prayer. Amen!

ANOTHER CRUCIAL STEP IN YOUR
HEALING JOURNEY IS TO BREAK
THE DEVASTATING POWER OF SECRETS.
IN THE NEXT CHAPTER YOU'LL LEARN
HOW TO UNDO THE SUFFOCATING
INFLUENCE OF SECRECY.

chapter 3

Secrets

SHHH! QUIET. HUSH. Secrets are the issue here. Some deeds are so despicable that the only sensible thing to do, so it would seem, is to forget they ever happened. Some pain is so great that the best thing to do, so it would seem, is to just bury it and *never* bring up the subject again. Keep it undercover. Maintain a code of silence. Be a good soldier. That's the best thing to do, right?

When the cool evening breezes were blowing, the man and his wife heard the Lord God walking about in the garden. So they hid from the Lord God among the trees. Then the Lord God called to the man, "Where are you?"

He replied, "I heard you walking in the garden, so I hid. I was afraid because I was naked."

"Who told you that you were naked?" the Lord God asked. "Have you eaten from the tree whose fruit I commanded you not to eat?"

—Genesis 3:8–11

Adam and Eve knew what it was like to have secrets. Not long after the newly created couple got a tour of their stress-free provisions in the garden of Eden, they decided to assert their independence from God. At that exact point, sin entered the human race. Adam and Eve took a bite from the fruit of the forbidden tree in defiance of the Father's instructions. God went looking for Adam. He asked Adam, "Where are you?" Adam and Eve both hid, covering themselves with fig leaves, when they heard God coming. They were naked and afraid.

Shame is an emotion that cries out "something is wrong with me."

Acting independently from God will have that effect on you. It will conjure up the skeletons in your closet. Sin and shame were born that day when Adam and Eve ate from the forbidden tree. Shame is an emotion that cries out "something is wrong with me." Shame makes you want to hide. Shame is a breeder of secrets.

Monica, a gifted graduate student, recently entered therapy. She and her family definitely bought into the notion of keeping secrets. When she was thirteen, her father began a tryst with her sister that lasted for several years. Incest! It was unspeakable. The secret remained safely tucked away until her father wanted to resume the affair in her sister's adult years. It was too much and big sister, Tammy, "spilled the beans."

The result was predictable. The truth came tumbling out. Mom and Dad got divorced, but even that was contained. Only the family knew the real reason. If the people in the community knew, scandal would have erupted. Dad was a civic leader, so they kept the whole matter a family secret. It was never reported to child protective services and the police were never contacted.

When Monica described it in therapy, she kept with the family code of silence. She understated the sadness of her story. She kept with the family tradition of secrecy. When she told her story, she minimized the seriousness of Dad's actions. She used non-provocative language and said, "Dad slept with Tammy." In our work together I pointed out that "slept with" sounded so calm and respectable, almost consensual. But the reality was quite different. When an adult has sex with a minor, the term is *rape*, not "slept with." When a father rapes his daughter, the word is *incest*.

You can become spiritually bankrupt if you allow the minions of trauma to silence you.

Rape and *incest* are unsettling words, but words that demand to be spoken, not swept quietly and unceremoniously under the rug. Giving an unmuffled voice to your story is an essential part of your healing journey. Trauma has a way of emptying out the ol' emotional bank account. You can become spiritually bankrupt if you allow the minions of trauma to silence you.

Secrecy is powerful. It keeps you cornered by your pain. Cut off. Shut off. Alienated. Estranged. Holding on to secrets keeps the burden of the responsibility on the sufferer, not on the one who created the suffering. Secrets maintain the status quo. They anchor you in *The Trauma Zone*. Secrecy is rooted in fear, isolation, and shame that fill you with emotional poison.

Fear preys on the core belief that nothing would be worse than telling the truth. The person who is controlled by his pain believes that the world would just fall apart if the truth were told. Actually, the opposite is the case. Fears fall apart when you face them. And in like manner, secrets lose their potency when you stand tall and tell your story. "The truth does not mind inspection" (sermon, Rev. Dr. Emmanuel Scott, ca. 1973). Shame is the hidden force behind secrets. But if we can stay focused, it becomes evident that when something horrible has happened to us—because of our own mistakes or someone else's—staying in our shame will *never* heal us. Transformation comes from breaking out of our prisons of isolation. We can ask for help. And we can receive the support we need. Getting the help that we need changes us profoundly. Secrets chain us to the past. We gain the strength to move forward by reaching out and breaking the silence that binds us. When we tell our story boldly, unashamedly, and in a safe place and with safe people, we are set free to fully reclaim our lives.

> *Secrets lose their potency when you stand tall and tell your story.*

ACTION STEPS

1. Ask yourself if there are important events in your journey out of *The Trauma Zone* that remain a secret to the person you have selected to support you.

2. Think prayerfully about what has been left out.

3. Request time from your selected support person that will not be rushed. Ask for at least an hour.

4. If the nature of your secret is something that is extremely upsetting to you, be sure to share it with a professional or someone you trust who has demonstrated experience at handling emotionally charged issues.

Let's Pray Together

Dear Lord, it is good to know that when it comes to secrets, silence is not golden. Today You are providing me with the tools to exit The Trauma Zone. Help me to understand that I may need to unload some secrets to leave behind the experiences that have weighed me down for so long. Give me wisdom and a discerning heart that I might make good choices concerning who I share my story with. Give me the right words, the right time, and the right place. Remove the spirit of fear that has kept me isolated. Give me the courage to face my secrets and boldly speak the truth. And by Your grace I will march forward. Amen.

NOW THAT YOU KNOW THAT THE
TRAUMA DJ CAN BE SILENCED, THAT
THE TRAUMA ZONE HAS EXIT SIGNS,
AND THAT THE WAY BEGINS WITH
BREAKING SECRETS, LET'S ADD TO YOUR
STRENGTH BY LOOKING AT HOW JESUS IS
OUR ROLE MODEL ON HOW TO HANDLE
OVERWHELMING STRESS.

chapter 4

Summary of **HOPE—**
Jesus Wrestled
with Trauma and Won

JESUS—THE STRONG, muscular, and wonder-
working Jesus—He's the one we love. Our affection is for the
Jesus who walked on water. Our affinity is for the Jesus who
fed five thousand folks with two fish and five barley loaves.
Our attraction is with the Jesus who could bend the laws of
nature and raise Lazarus from the dead. We are drawn to the
Jesus who opened blind eyes, unstopped deaf ears, and restored withered limbs. A Jesus with some exploits. A Jesus
with some trophies. That Jesus could have been King of the
Jews. That Jesus could have single-handedly toppled the
Roman Empire. He's the Jesus we want.

And if the truth be told, we would rewrite some of the script
if we could. We are a power-hungry lot, so some of us would
take out the section where Jesus came into Jerusalem on the first
Palm Sunday riding on the colt of a donkey. Instead, we would
put Jesus on a big white stallion and have Him ride into the city
with style. We would be comfortable with that Jesus, one with
power and an attitude to boot.

Yet it was our weaknesses he carried; it was our
sorrows that weighed him down. And we thought his
troubles were a punishment from God, a punishment
for his own sins! But he was pierced for our rebellion,
crushed for our sins. He was beaten so we could be
whole. He was whipped so we could be healed. All of
us, like sheep, have strayed away. We have left God's
paths to follow our own. Yet the Lord laid
on him the sins of us all.

—Isaiah 53:4–6

The Jesus we like to brag about is the one who could walk on water. The Suffering Servant is often left to fend for Himself. Peter was arguably Jesus' most outspoken supporter. But when it came to suffering, it was "every man for himself." Jesus was left to bear the cross by Himself. The memorable passage in Isaiah 53:4–6 outlines for us the enormous hardship the Messiah would have to bear. His power was remarkably balanced by His passion for service. His willingness to suffer on our behalf demonstrates His commitment to our growth. His willingness to put Himself on the altar for the Father shows that He is worthy of our faithful allegiance.

To appreciate Jesus we must understand and embrace His humanity as well.

Jesus understood that we would struggle with accepting all of Him. Jesus' powerful side is only half of the good news. Why stop at half of the story? To appreciate Jesus we must understand and embrace His humanity as well. It is this hungry, thirsty, exhausted, bleeding, and dying Jesus that unpackaged the wonder of His humanity. The vulnerable, suffering Jesus makes us uncomfortable. Jesus the meek sounds like Jesus the weak. We don't like this humility stuff. You know, "Turn the other cheek." We'd prefer a Jesus who said, "If somebody messes with you, deck 'em." But that's not what the Master taught us.

It is Jesus' ability to sacrifice so much of His power and function like an ordinary human that gives the rest of us earth-bound residents so much hope. Jesus allowed Himself to be bound by our rules while He walked the earth. He got tired like the rest of us. He got hungry like the rest of us. He didn't beam Himself from town to town as He preached. He walked hot, dusty roads just like His disciples had to walk them. He didn't have angels fan Him and feed Him grapes. And He suffered through hardship like the rest of us. But it is what Jesus did with His pain that shines through for us like the morning sun and gives us hope.

Jesus experienced trauma without being traumatized.

The mystery is that Jesus takes His own brokenness and transforms it into strength. By looking at how Jesus handled trouble we are provided with a road map for exiting our own trauma zone. We can follow His example. Jesus experienced trauma without being traumatized. And because Jesus did it, we can too.

A personal testimony seems in order here. My eighty-three-year-old mother and ninety-five-year-old uncle, now decreased, lived in a row home in Philadelphia. Unfortunately, their former next-door neighbor was psychotic. She had been living in her home without running water or electricity for several years. According to neighbors, she had been allowing a crack addict to stay with her some evenings. Neighbors believed she would hide drugs in the dilapidated house. One day two drug dealers demanded access to the neighbor's house. The neighbor refused and the men firebombed the house. In a matter of minutes, the neighbor's and my mother's house were fully engulfed in flames. And just like that, my mom and uncle were homeless.

But something wonderful happened. My wife and I were out of town at the time of the fire. But within minutes, my daughter Darielle arrived at my mom's house and provided support. Members of my church picked up my family, comforted them, and offered them practical support. My mother's church family was very generous and encouraging. My wife and I invited them to stay with us. And the end result was that they felt loved and cared for, and began looking forward to moving into a new home closer to us. Mom and Uncle Rufus, like Jesus, experienced trauma without being traumatized.

Jesus was always clear that no matter what happened, God was in control.

Jesus suffered. Make no mistake about it. But let's look at how He handled His challenges and take some notes from the Master.

The most stressful time Jesus faced on earth was when He confronted the prospect of His own death. He knew He was going to be betrayed by the men He ate and lived with every day. Has one person you trusted ever betrayed you? Well, multiply it twelve times (once for each disciple) and you get a flavor for what it must have felt like for Jesus.

The apprehension with which Jesus approached His crucifixion made perfect sense. He knew He would be tortured. He knew He would be betrayed. He knew He had to bear the cross alone. Yet, Jesus had a handle on coping strategies two thousand years ago that we are just now learning to prove in the behavioral sciences. Jesus coped by using the following:

ACTION STEPS:

1. **Reaching Up.** Jesus remained connected to God at all times. He never acted independently from God. The Father was His source. Jesus realized that there is only one sin—*pride*. Pride influences a person to act independently from God. Pride creates the breeding ground for every evil that affects us all. Jesus was wise enough to never become so full of Himself that He forgot who sent Him here in the first place. He said, "My nourishment comes from doing the will of God, who sent me, and from finishing his work" (John 4:34). Jesus was able to cope with enormous pain, even His own death, because He relied on God to guide and strengthen Him.

2. **Reaching Out.** Lone Rangers do poorly when stressed. In the garden of Gethsemane Jesus asked His three closest disciples to "keep watch and pray" (Mark 14:38) as He prayed through the night. Jesus created a circle of support to help at His most difficult hour. Now, the record shows that Jesus' support team all went to sleep on Him. But God never promised us perfect support from people. Allowing God to be your source gives you a cushion. People will let you down sometimes; but that's all right, because some people will come through for you. And where family and friends fall short, God will make up the difference. We were created for community.

3. **Put On Your "Faith Glasses."** What you believe about trouble makes a world of difference in your ability to handle a potentially traumatizing situation. Jesus was always clear that no matter what happened, God was in control. This does not mean that unfortunate and even tragic things won't happen to us. But God being

in control means that when it's all said and done, *He has the final word, not your trouble.* And that's mighty good news. Looking at your problems through the lens of faith gives you an advantage. It develops in you the mind-set of Jesus, the Christ. You become aware that although life circumstances may at times be unfair, God is in the midst of your pain bringing out good.

The psalmist wrote, "Weeping may last through the night, but joy comes with the morning" (Psalm 30:5). When you believe that God is in the midst of your trials, it helps you to stay out of victimlike, helpless modes of thinking. Instead, you can say to yourself with confidence the words of the Apostle Paul: "And we know that God causes everything to work together for the good of those who love God and are called according to his purpose for them" (Romans 8:28). God is in the midst of pain bringing out good. He is developing our character so that we can make better choices and experience His peace.

Let's Pray Together

Dear Lord, when You walked the earth You did many wonderful things. You worked mind-boggling miracles. But the greatest miracle was for You to reveal Your humanity. In Your flesh You showed how much You loved me. You loved me enough to be nailed to a cross. You loved me enough to allow a crown of thorns to be pressed into Your brow. You loved me enough to die for my sins.

Help me today, Lord, to realize that with Your help I can transform my thinking. I can handle my problems the way You handled Yours. I can learn to believe that nothing is too hard for You. When I face my trials, I can remember that because of Your resurrection I can bring that same power into my everyday life situations. I don't have to let my troubles have the last say; that honor belongs to You. You have the final say, Lord. You are in control. And because You are my source, I am at peace. Amen.

NOW THAT YOU SEE HOW JESUS OVERCAME HIS TRAUMA, YOU KNOW THAT YOU CAN DO THE SAME. EQUIPPED WITH RESURRECTION FAITH YOU CAN FACE *THE TRAUMA ZONE*. THE FIRST TRAUMA STATION IS THE "CAN'T COPE WITH YOUR EMOTIONS" STATION. IT IS FOUNDATIONAL TO UNDERSTANDING ALL OF THE OTHER TRAUMA STATIONS. YOU ARE READY. LET'S FACE THE MONSTERS TOGETHER.

Can't Cope with Your Emotions

Emotional trauma stirs up extreme reactions to life circumstances. Sometimes the response is paralyzing fear. At other times it could be depression, anxiety, or rage that rises to the surface. But the good news is that you can regain control of your emotions in the aftermath of traumatic life experiences. The chapters that follow provide practical guidance for calming distressful feelings.

chapter 5

Emotional Roller **COASTER**

I NEVER COULD STAND roller coaster rides. You know the routine. First you are soaring into a blue sky. Then, before you know it, the bottom falls out. You are gunning for the ground. You see it: grass and dirt. You feel it: the wind is pulsating against your face. Mouth wide open. Heart pounding. Blood rushing. Screaming as loud as you can. The response is automatic. Visceral. Not my idea of fun. Not my idea of an adrenaline rush. Just doesn't agree with the ol' stomach. So when the kids (grandkids that is, and I have seven) ask me if I want to go with them on a roller coaster ride, I just smile and say, "Go ahead. I'll watch you." Although I'm trying not to let on that I would be shaking in my boots if I went on the ride with them, I think they know. Pop-Pop punked out.

In many ways, going through a traumatic experience is like being on a roller coaster ride. Your life feels up in the air. Lots of ups and downs. Lots of sudden turns. Lots of misdirection and uncertainty. Emotional pain feels the same way: like a roller coaster ride into oblivion—a ride that never ends, so it seems.

The Master understood the importance of being grounded

and calm. Before He finished His earthly ministry He gave His disciples powerful instructions about staying anchored to His love in the midst of unsettling times. Listen to His conversation with the disciples:

"I am telling you these things now while I am still with you. But when the Father sends the Advocate as my representative—that is, the Holy Spirit— he will teach you everything and will remind you of everything I have told you.

"I am leaving you with a gift—peace of mind and heart. And the peace I give is a gift the world cannot give. So don't be troubled or afraid.

"I have told you all this so that you may have peace in me. Here on earth you will have many trials and sorrows. But take heart, because I have overcome the world."

—John 14:25–27; 16:33

It's the perception that hard emotional times never end that makes the experience appear so unmanageable.

If anyone knew what it was like to be on an emotional roller coaster, it was Jesus. One minute He was being hailed, and the next He was being nailed. Within a week, His disciples deserted Him, Judas betrayed Him, Peter denied Him, the Sanhedrin condemned Him, an angry crowd mocked Him, and the Romans crucified Him. People can be mean-hearted and wildly unpredictable. And if you let them, they'll send you on an emotional roller coaster ride.

As Jesus prepared to return to heaven, He gave His followers a "heads up." He said, "Here on earth you will have many trials and sorrows" (John 16:33). He also told them to take courage because His ability to create peace is greater than the evil one's ability to stir up turmoil. In short—don't be intimidated.

It's the perception that hard emotional times never end that makes the experience appear so unmanageable. When there seems to be no end to your suffering, it is easy to become overwhelmed. Your mind plays tricks on you. Reason goes out the window. Calmer heads don't prevail. Instead, panic prevails. That's what distress can do to you. You slide into *The Trauma Zone*—a place where the rules of logic are suspended and raw emotions rule. Fear takes over. You can't function. Due to the emotional pain you have labored through, you are not level-headed, reasonable, cool, calm, or collected. There is a domino effect that kicks into action when you are being flooded with stress. The upshot is that you can't cope with your emotions.

Sometimes you may respond to what feels like an attack by overreacting and "losing it." The overreactor's credo is to fight fire with fire. Get them before they get you. The other way you respond to your trauma is through distancing. You numb your feelings by hitting the emotional off switch. As a brave but weather-beaten soul, you go through your life unmoved by your own pain or the heartache of others. You become unavailable as a way of coping.

The response to being overwhelmed and unable to cope with your feelings is central to understanding trauma and the role of every other trauma station. You may have memories of events that occurred long ago that seem as if they are happening all over again right now. This happens through nightmares, flashbacks, and intrusive thoughts (Can't Tell Time). Your life may become stagnant for years and not make much progress (Can't Move). You may keep on making the same mistakes, personally and professionally (Can't Learn), and minimize the severity of your predicament via denial (Can't See).

Overreacting

is a choice, but

so is poise.

When all of this happens, common sense takes the backseat. The Trauma DJ puts in the tape and whispers in our ears, "It's never going to get better." So we react with "fight or flight." Each trauma station is a creative way our mind adapts to what appears to be an overpowering situation. But deep inside, we already know intuitively that the steady diet of negativity the Trauma DJ serves us keeps us locked in *The Trauma Zone.*

The good news is that our lives can get much better. God has provided a strategy of escape for us. And the way is coping. Overreacting is a choice, but so is poise. With God's help and the support of our loved ones, we can face unbelievable stress with the astonishing peace of God, which "exceeds anything we can understand" (Philippians 4:7). We can get off the roller coaster ride and stand on solid ground when we ask the Master to give us His amazing grace.

And I am convinced that nothing can ever separate us from God's love. Neither death nor life, neither angels nor demons, neither our fears for today nor our worries about tomorrow—not even the powers of hell can separate us from God's love. No power in the sky above or in the earth below—indeed, nothing in all creation will ever be able to separate us from the love of God that is revealed in Christ Jesus our Lord.

—Romans 8:38–39

Peace and grace are powerful weapons against stress. In the New Testament, a Koine Greek word that is frequently used for peace is *irene*. It means balance, beauty, harmony, symmetry, and order. God's peace translates practically into changing the way we think about our trials. We shift from believing that we are hapless victims of circumstance, controlled by heartless fate or mindless people. Instead, we begin to believe that despite the damaging experiences we have encountered, we are not "damaged goods." We are children of the Most High. We are loved unconditionally by Him. I have found Philip Yancey's definition helpful: "There is nothing that we can do to make God love us any more, and there is nothing that we can do that will make God love us any less."

God's unconditional love gives birth to His wonderful peace that keeps us, sustains us, and gives our lives focus.

God's unconditional love gives birth to His wonderful peace that keeps us, sustains us, and gives our lives focus. With focus we realize that our life has purpose, even in our tragedies. Just ask Malik. He has quite a testimony. He has learned the secret of transforming tragedies into triumphs.

Malik is a sixty-one-year-old decorated Vietnam vet, a pilot who experienced his worst trauma at the hands of his family. He was cruelly molested as a toddler, and he suffered emotional abuse from his first wife that left him deeply scarred. Long after the divorce, she still seemed bent on getting everything from him that she could. She committed identity theft and took out a loan using Malik's name. As a result of his accumulated pain, Malik experienced a crisis of faith.

Before Malik found the exit signs to *The Trauma Zone*,

life appeared so bleak he felt God had forsaken him. Malik was angry—with God and people. He didn't know who he could trust. He felt trapped in his pain with no way out. His life seemed hopeless. Groping for light, he experienced a lunar eclipse of the soul.

But with newfound love and support in his second marriage, and with hard work in therapy, Malik began his march out of *The Trauma Zone*. One of the first steps was realizing that much of his pain was something he was allowing to perpetuate through his negative thinking. For example, he expected the worst from people. He kept his defenses up, even with people who loved him.

Bit by bit Malik became aware that the losses he experienced previously were real. At the same time, he learned that the consistent love he received from his new family was also real and something he could count on. Gradually, a new skill emerged— moderation. With support, he no longer was driven from "pillar to post" on a wild emotional roller coaster ride.

Malik is enjoying his life now. Problems still pop up, but now he manages them as they happen with much greater calm. And the biggest reason is that he changed the way he thinks. This trauma survivor wanted to break free from the isolation that kept him chained and bound to *The Trauma Zone*. He realized he had much more power than he thought he had. He came to learn that with God's help he could make healthy choices that would transform his tragedies into triumphs.

Like Malik, we too can find hope even in our darkest moments. If we keep looking to the Lord, we discover that just as the eclipse passes, so do our troubles. We discern that with patience and with choosing to use our own God-given power, we can get off the emotional roller coaster and learn to cope with our emotions.

ACTION STEPS

1. **Cultivate coping skills.**

   ⮑Relax in God's grace.

   ⮑Do your best and remember that God is with you.

   ⮑Focus your energy toward solving the issue at hand rather than reacting with intense emotions.

   ⮑Remember that worry, panic, and rage are useless emotions.

   ⮑Respond to today's challenges with a calm decisiveness, anchored in your faith, that God is with you in every trial you face.

2. **Think of one event in the past several days or weeks where you "lost it."** How could you have better handled the situation?

3. **When pressures mount, try memorizing these brief Scriptures on peace:**

   Don't worry about anything; instead, pray about everything. Tell God what you need, and thank him for all he has done. Then you will experience God's peace, which exceeds anything we can understand. His peace will guard your hearts and minds as you live in Christ Jesus.—PHILIPPIANS 4:6–7

   You will keep in perfect peace all who trust in you, all whose thoughts are fixed on you!—ISAIAH 26:3

4. **Choose to live in God's peace.** Think about one challenge you are facing. Ask yourself what changes you need to make in your thinking to better cope with your emotions.

Let's Pray Together

Blessed Lord, You know all things. You created me. And You know exactly what I need. I acknowledge that there are times when my trials get the best of me. Sometimes I doubt that things will get better. But that's just my pain speaking to me. There is a higher road that I can follow. There is a wiser voice, deep down on the inside, I can choose to listen to. It's Your voice, Lord. It's a voice that counsels me to relax. It's a voice that lets me know that although my trouble sometimes feels like a roller coaster ride, I have options.

One day at a time, I can change the way I think. I can transform the way I respond to the challenges that confront me. I can temper my emotions with knowledge, discernment, and truth. I can choose not to be afraid and not to live life on the edge by choosing instead the gift of Your peace. Amen.

NOW THAT WE KNOW THAT DEVELOPING COPING SKILLS IS A POWERFUL ANSWER TO THE TENDENCY OF TRAUMATIZED FOLK TO OVERREACT OR UNDERRESPOND, LET'S LOOK TOGETHER AT THE CHILDREN'S STORY OF *CHICKEN LITTLE* AND HOW THAT SIMPLE TALE HELPS US UNDERSTAND ANOTHER CRUCIAL ASPECT OF RECOVERING FROM TRAUMA—CLOSURE.

chapter 6

The Sky Is **FALLING**

WE ALL KNOW WHAT IT FEELS LIKE to be overwhelmed and at the breaking point. But the fairy tale character Chicken Little said it best. "The sky is falling; the sky is falling." Chicken Little had stumbled into *The Trauma Zone*.

The account of Chicken Little is only a fairy tale, but her story is relevant to people in *The Trauma Zone*. Faced with an overwhelming sense of impending doom, you too may feel that the sky is falling. And when you have been through a terrible storm, at times it feels like there will be a storm every day.

Jesus and the disciples had their share of storms and up-sets. Let's look at how Jesus responded to one of His storms:

But soon a fierce storm came up. High waves were breaking into the boat, and it began to fill with water.

Jesus was sleeping at the back of the boat with his head on a cushion. The disciples woke him up, shouting, "Teacher, don't you care that we're going to drown?"

When Jesus woke up, he rebuked the wind and said to the water, "Silence! Be still!" Suddenly the wind stopped, and there was a great calm.

—Mark 4:37–39

The Sea of Galilee was known for fierce windstorms that often threatened to capsize the small fishing boats that sailed its waters. Even experienced fishermen like Peter and Andrew, James and John respected and feared the fury of these unpredictable storms. Ironically, on one stormy day, Jesus decided to catch up on some sleep.

On the surface, Jesus seemed strangely detached from His disciples. They watched the storm develop while Jesus slept. They were worried. Frightened. They weren't interested in seeing what heaven looked like on that day. And so, they woke the Master. Over the howling wind they shouted, "Don't You care about us?" Jesus faced the storm and commanded it to be still. The wind and the waves obeyed. There was instant calm.

We can talk back to our inner tempests and find calm in the midst of turmoil and upheaval.

Jesus has passed on to us this same authority. Although we cannot challenge a physical hurricane, we can talk back to our inner tempests and find calm in the midst of turmoil and upheaval. We can speak peace to the howling winds of emotional pain and despair.

On the other side of the storm is hope. Bringing us through our tragedies and life disappointments is what Jesus does best. Recovery is God's answer to our pain. Our trauma may have knocked us down, but we don't have to stay down. Recovery does something incredibly powerful. While on the one hand we can acknowledge that something horrific has happened in our lives, we can also affirm that God's love for us is stronger than our trauma.

In the fall of 2004 a series of hurricanes tortured Florida and large portions of the southern United States and the Caribbean. The storms brought with them widespread death and destruction. When the hurricane warnings went up, it was normal to become alarmed. Many people boarded up their windows and were forced to evacuate. But to continue in the alert mode after the hurricane was over would no longer serve a purpose.

The good news about posttraumatic stress is the "post."

The good news about posttraumatic stress is the "post." The word *post* suggests that the trauma is over. The danger is over. We are now in a new "after the storm" phase of things. This is great news. During the storm the wisest thing to do is to take refuge. Find shelter. Call for help. Dial 911. Cleaning up during a storm is dangerous. But after the storm, we assess the damage and start putting the pieces of our lives back together again.

One of the most important needs in recovery from trauma is to realize when we need to shift our energy from taking cover to taking charge. Now that the danger is over, we need to mobilize the "cleanup" operation.

Just ask Linda, a gifted professional woman and courageous trauma survivor I worked with in therapy. Linda recounted horror stories of her childhood abuse. When she was in middle school, she was assaulted by her cousin who lived with her family.

When a person goes through years of this kind of abuse, it has a profound effect on self-esteem. Linda told me how difficult it was for her to receive feedback from her friends whenever there was a conflict. Any disagreement felt like a searing attack. When she shared what her friends said to her, it was more like an acorn falling from a tree than a bomb falling from the air.

As Linda and I worked together, she began to see that the storm was over—that the sky was not falling. As a result, she was able to begin picking up the pieces and to move on with her life.

You can too!

ACTION STEPS ▾

1. **Focus on one thing that is overwhelming you right now.**

2. **Name one positive action you can take to remedy this problem.**

3. **Who in your circle of support can you call on to assist you?**

4. **Ask God for wisdom in finding a solution to your challenge.**

Let's Pray Together

Thank You, Jesus, for being the calmer of my storms. Because You are in the boat with me, I no longer have to be overwhelmed. You can tell my storms to "hush now," and the winds of my life will obey. So replace my fear that "the sky is falling" with faith that You are in control. Help me today to relax in Your love. Amen.

THE NEXT STOP ON OUR HEALING
JOURNEY IS LEARNING HOW TO AVOID
THE PITFALL OF BEING FRAGILE
AS A RESULT OF OUR TRAUMA. MANY
SURVIVORS BECOME EASILY OFFENDED
AND DISCOURAGED. THE NEXT CHAPTER
TELLS THE STORY OF PEOPLE WHO
REALIZED THAT THEIR TRAUMA WAS
PROMPTING THEM TO OVERREACT TO
THE CHALLENGES THEY WERE FACING.
AS YOU TUNE IN, PERHAPS YOU WILL
DISCOVER THAT THEIR STORY IS
IN PART YOUR STORY TOO.

Trigger-**HAPPY**

TRAUMA MAKES YOU VULNERABLE. You feel naked. Exposed. You know it. And others can sense it too. It could be the hesitancy in your decisions. It could be the look in your eyes. It could be the quaver in your voice. Or it could be the "dead giveaway" that your confidence has become shaky.

Sometimes, being trigger-happy means that you are quick to blame yourself for your suffering. You sense that your vulnerability is an open book and you don't like it one bit. You sense that someone, anyone, is going to pounce on you. Living with emotional trauma is often like waking up feeling backed into a corner. You know the old saying, "The best defense is a good offense." It fits here. So you come out in your best kung fu stance and let out a good martial arts shout in the hope that it might ward off would-be attackers.

You attack first. You become trigger-happy. When people speak, you make sure you get your point in first. You become easily offended or hurt by something someone says because you often don't slow down enough to get the whole story. When you hear people whispering, you often end up jumping to conclusions, convinced that they're whispering about something you've said or done. People like that deserve a good dose of the evil eye, right?

> *The effect of our being wounded is that we work overtime not to get injured again.*

The effect of our being wounded is that we work overtime not to get injured again. It makes perfect sense. It's just that being on guard most of the time makes it hard to develop close relationships because so much of our energy is spent wondering what someone has "up their sleeve." Thankfully, our pain doesn't have to organize our relationships forever. We can change our scripts.

The Bible offers us a wonderful illustration of a person who was trigger-happy but who with God's help was able to change his script.

Peter was always the disciple who was most vocal about his support for Jesus. Even at the Last Supper, when Jesus said that He would be betrayed, it was Peter who said that he would *never* let Jesus down. Let's listen to how Peter handled the pressure when Jesus was arrested and someone in the crowd recognized him as one of Jesus' disciples:

> *So they arrested him and led him to the high priest's home. And Peter followed at a distance.*
>
> *The guards lit a fire in the middle of the courtyard and sat around it, and Peter joined them there.*
>
> *A servant girl noticed him in the firelight and began staring at him. Finally she said, "This man was one of Jesus' followers!"*

*But Peter denied it. "Woman," he said,
"I don't even know him!"*

*After a while someone else looked at him and said,
"You must be one of them!"*

"No, man, I'm not!" Peter retorted.

*About an hour later someone else insisted, "This must
be one of them, because he is a Galilean, too."*

*But Peter said, "Man, I don't know what you are
talking about." And immediately, while he was
still speaking, the rooster crowed.*

*At that moment the Lord turned and looked at Peter.
Then Peter remembered that the Lord had said, "Before the rooster crows tomorrow morning, you will
deny three times that you even know me."*

And Peter left the courtyard, weeping bitterly.

—Luke 22:54–62

Can you imagine how utterly ashamed and lonely Peter must have felt when he realized that he had just betrayed the Son of God? It played out just as Jesus said it would. Peter probably wanted to find a huge rock and crawl under it for the rest of his life. Usually it was so easy for him to speak up for Jesus. But in the clutch, Peter choked.

Being in The Trauma Zone *is about living your life under the gun.*

The good news is that Peter's denial of Christ in the courtyard is not the end of the story. Over time, Peter learned how to be courageous under fire. He learned not to overreact in a spirit of fear but to speak his truth clearly and passionately.

Peter learned to maintain his composure whether he was being cheered or jeered.

One aspect of trauma is to react like Peter did in the face of personal pain. Survivors know this kind of pressure. We have endured experiences in which our lives may have taken a tragic turn because we just didn't react quickly enough. Perhaps we live under a cloud of permanent regret in which our Trauma DJ points an accusing finger and says, "If only you had responded more quickly, your whole life would have turned out differently."

Being in *The Trauma Zone* is about living your life under the gun. Just ask Renee, who is a survivor of domestic violence. Afterward, she had a hard time trusting men. When she began dating, if a gentleman gave even the slightest hint of being controlling, he was history.

In therapy, we talked about Renee taunting her trauma. This means that you face the thing that you fear the most. Sometimes it means finding something humorous about how you handle or view your situation. Renee did this when she thought of how quickly she learned to dump a guy if she felt uncomfortable with him. As we worked together, she learned to slow down her reactions to people and enjoy the moment more. She even learned to laugh at her former pattern of letting a relationship go at the first sign of trouble. She gave herself the nickname of "Quick Draw McGraw." I knew she was getting much better when she e-mailed me one day and the letter had at the top a picture of the cartoon character Quick Draw.

Renee learned to be more patient and not to be afraid of aggressive men or of being vulnerable enough to love when the right opportunity arose. With this growth she started dating again. Now she is able to joke that her new date is going well; but if he ever "steps out of line," he'll have to deal with "Quick Draw."

ACTION STEPS

1. **Take a deep breath.** It is normal to react strongly to the threat of harm. But remember, the nature of trauma is that you respond to situations as though you are in danger when there really is no threat. Trauma sounds a lot of false alarms. So learn to follow your instincts as to when to invite people into your space and when to keep them at bay.

2. **Learn from your mistakes.** Pay special attention to your reaction track record. Note when your read on people and situations is on the money and also note any patterns that stand out when you read people incorrectly. Remember those situations and make adjustments accordingly.

3. **Remember that God is your source so that when people occasionally don't come through for you it is not a shock to your system.** Instead, you can be steady and calm because you know that God loves you and that He will sustain you through any situation you can face. That's mighty good to know!

Let's Pray Together

Dear Lord, there are times when I feel under the gun. There are moments when I feel afraid and that I have to take things into my own hands in order to be safe. At those times remind me, Lord, that the only safety is in You. Help me to trust You more. Help me to trust Your Spirit that is inside of me—Your Spirit who leads me to let go of the trigger finger and to hold on to Your promise that You are with me regardless of the circumstances. With You inside me, surrounding me with Your love, I

*can face anything. I can respond thoughtfully and prayer-
fully to my life rather than react impulsively and fearfully.
Today I step out on the comfort of Your promise that You
are with me and I am at peace. Amen.*

NEXT, LET'S TALK TOGETHER ABOUT THE
ISSUE OF SHAME AND HOW PEOPLE WHO
HAVE BEEN THROUGH EXCESSIVE
TURMOIL TEND TO FEEL VULNERABLE
BECAUSE OF PERCEIVED FAULTS THAT
FEEL LIKE OPEN WOUNDS. I CALL
THEM "SHAME BUTTONS."

Shame **BUTTONS**

NO MATTER HOW HARD WE TRY, perfection escapes us. But that doesn't stop us from fantasizing. So we imagine. We ponder what it would be like to have a slice of perfection: a soul mate by our side, children who listen and volunteer to wash the dishes and do their homework without prompting, a job we enjoy so much that we look forward to work, a car that makes heads turn (and not because the muffler just fell off), and a bank account strong enough that the initials NSF (non-sufficient funds) are never stamped on our checks. Sounds sweet, right? Now pinch yourself, it's time for a reality check.

Those of us who are walking through the valley of trauma are dreamers. We yearn for a life that is much better than the one that served us a platter of emotional turmoil. We just want better. We long for perfection or at least what we *think* is perfection. But when we hunger for perfection, we become famished for the unattainable.

Our suffering pushes us to seek extreme solutions, and perfection is an extreme. It's an attempt by our soul to purge itself from its close encounter with evil. We've found ourselves peering deeply into the ugly side of life and have been flattened by it. Our pain has made us feel like roadkill run over by an eighteen-wheeler. We have experienced people at their worst. We have endured so much selfishness and callousness that it takes all of our energy to keep it together.

The problem is that the search for perfection results in shame. Perfectionism will leave you full of toxic shame. It is an emotion that says you are defective. John Bradshaw in *Healing the Shame that Binds You* (Deerfield Beach, Florida: Health Communications, 2005) says people who are shame-based teeter toward either perfectionism on the one hand or inferiority on the other.

The problem is that the search for perfection results in shame.

The Trauma DJ has a real field day with toxic shame. The voice within becomes an inner brute. When you don't do everything just right, the Trauma DJ barks out criticism: "I don't believe you messed that up again." Ordinary mistakes can evoke a shame attack. And the target of the shame attack is invariably the same. It's you! The tragedy of shame is that it is harsh and often unforgiving. Shame turns you against yourself. It either sets the bar so high that no human could reach the goal or sets it so low that it strips your humanity.

Just ask Yolanda, a talented businesswoman who is a warm and generous soul. When we worked together, she frequently talked about not feeling good about herself and her accomplishments. Invariably, the culprit behind her diminished self-esteem was her earnest desire to get everything right. I would gently remind her that balancing her recovery from an emotionally abusive childhood and her multiple roles as wife, mom, and career woman required considerable time and nurture. Her tendency toward perfectionism set her up for endless disappointments because no one can achieve perfection.

I've observed that people who have been beaten down by the Trauma DJ's overbearing critique are filled with so much shame that they want to quit.

The apostle Peter nearly gave up. After he denied Jesus, he probably felt totally useless. He left the ministry and returned to his more familiar work as a fisherman. Let's listen to how Jesus both consoles and challenges His friend Peter:

> *People who have been beaten down by the Trauma DJ's overbearing critique are filled with so much shame that they want to quit.*

After breakfast Jesus asked Simon Peter, "Simon son of John, do you love me more than these?"
"Yes, Lord," Peter replied, "you know I love you."
"Then feed my lambs," Jesus told him.
Jesus repeated the question:
"Simon son of John, do you love me?"
"Yes, Lord," Peter said, "you know I love you."
"Then take care of my sheep," Jesus said.
A third time he asked him,
"Simon son of John, do you love me?"
Peter was hurt that Jesus asked the question a third time. He said, "Lord, you know everything. You know that I love you."

Jesus said, "Then feed my sheep."
—John 21:15–17

Jesus understood exactly what was required. Peter needed to be drained of his shame. So the post-resurrection Christ interviewed Peter, and in the conversation, the Master laid out a plan for Peter's restoration. Jesus' line of questions made Peter squirm. When Jesus asked Peter three times if he loved Him, it was intentionally designed to match the three times Peter denied Him. Peter was embarrassed with Jesus' inquiry. But it was necessary. Jesus forced Peter to face his failure so that he could grow from his mistake.

Shame makes you want to hide. Jesus could not use a Peter who was hiding out. Jesus needed a Peter who was willing to stand out. Jesus needed a Peter who was so grounded in his allegiance to Him that He could send him out to the world as a witness of His marvelous love. The good news is that Peter worked through his shame. Because he did, he became an integral part of the spread of the gospel in the first-century church.

It is a good thing that Jesus did not seek out perfect followers. If Jesus were a perfectionist, He would have assembled the scholarly, the connected, the wealthy, and the powerful as His followers. Instead, the Master surrounded Himself with a ragtag group of hot-tempered, cussin' disciples to spread the gospel for Him.

Of course we know that the people God chooses are different from the ones He uses. He fixes us. He changes us. He gives us a story that He personally edits. He cuts out perfection and shame, and He pastes in excellence and grace. We begin a whole new journey with Him—one that is gentle, balanced, fruitful, and driven by the life-transforming power of His love.

ACTION STEPS

1. **Perfectionism leaves you with a life full of shame.** Are you a perfectionist? If so, give yourself a gentleness break.

2. **When you are feeling fear and shame, a wonderful verse of Scripture to recite is Psalm 27:1:**

   The Lord is my light and my salvation—so why should I be afraid? The Lord is my fortress, protecting me from danger, so why should I tremble?

   Try memorizing this verse; and when you are confronted with intimidating life circumstances, remember that the Lord is the source of your strength. Be encouraged. God has the final say.

3. **Don't let your shame button work.**

   ⮑When your Trauma DJ gives you the drill about how you messed up, just relax and say to yourself, "I might be imperfect but so are the other six billion people who populate the globe." Get sassy and then stick out your tongue. (Be sure no one is around you!)

   ⮑Make sure you don't take yourself too seriously. Laugh at yourself daily—in a loving, not ridiculing, way.

Let's Pray Together

Dear Lord, I admit that I have my shame buttons. Give me the strength today to face my failures with patience and my disappointments with grace. Help me always to remember that I am not a mistake but that I am Your child. Thank You for preparing me to do Your work. Amen.

AN IMPORTANT PART OF DOING GOD'S
WORK IS TO REMEMBER THAT THE LORD
GETS THE GLORY OUT OF OUR LIVES
WHEN WE LEARN TO COPE BETTER WITH
OUR REACTIONS TO LIFE CHALLENGES.
THE NEXT CHAPTER CAPTURES SOME OF
THE IMPORTANT SKILLS NEEDED TO
MANAGE OUR STRESS MORE EFFECTIVELY.
LET'S TUNE IN TOGETHER.

chapter 9

Summary of **HOPE**— You Can Cope

EMOTIONAL TRAUMA IS A THIEF. It steals your ability to keep your feelings in check. The intensity of your emotional pain robs you of your capacity to respond to people and incidents calmly. Trauma pushes you to your limit. You find yourself on the edge. Sometimes you feel shoved over the edge into an inner world where your feelings scream at you—anger becomes rage, fear turns into panic, and disappointments morph into depression. At other times your feelings simply stare you down in stunned silence because it hurts too much to feel.

This is an old problem. As long as there have been people who trusted in God, there has been adversity that has tested us. And the hardships are not just from flesh and blood enemies. We have learned along the way, though, that there is hope and help for the journey. This hope is stronger than the pain inflicted on us by people who are uncaring and thoughtless.

King David has written some classic songs (which we call psalms) that capture the rich hope of our faith. Soak in the words of the psalmist:

The Lord is my shepherd; I have all that I need.

He lets me rest in green meadows;
He leads me beside peaceful streams.

He renews my strength.

He guides me along right paths,
bringing honor to his name.

Even when I walk through the darkest valley,
I will not be afraid, for you are close beside me.

Your rod and your staff protect and comfort me.

You prepare a feast for me
in the presence of my enemies.

You honor me by anointing my head with oil.

My cup overflows with blessings.

Surely your goodness and unfailing love will
pursue me all the days of my life, and I will
live in the house of the Lord forever.

—Psalm 23

One of the gifts of this passage is that it teaches us not to be intimidated by those who seek to harm us because God is protecting us. Now, God's protection does not mean no evil will befall us. It certainly does not mean that we will escape difficult trials and grueling tests. Instead, it affirms that God is always with us regardless of what happens. We learn to protect ourselves by including different people in our inner circle and keeping destructive people at bay. If the destructive ones are already in our lives, we escort them out until they make a commitment to change.

> *God is always with us regardless of what happens.*

As we reflect together on Psalm 23, it is reassuring to think of God as our own personal shepherd. His watchful eye and nurturing hand are perfect medicine for people who have been traumatized. One of the chief things that happens to you when you have come through trauma is that you become uptight, typically about many things. But the path of recovery helps you to relax and enjoy your life, perhaps for the first time.

There comes a time when we can settle the old account of pain through our faith.

Rather than our emotions being in a constant state of flux in which we feel out of control, out of sorts, and out of line, our hearts are transformed by the Shepherd's love and we take our emotions back. Instead of our feelings ruling us, we learn to cope with our emotions by relying on God's love in any situation, pleasant or unpleasant. In His love we can rest in His peace that has been so elusive to us.

Just ask Naomi, a gifted surgeon who grew up in a family where there was rage and violence. The effects of her experience left her with chronic depression in adulthood. In fact, Naomi shared that she was depressed for twenty years. When she came to treatment, she was on depression medication. She gained a fresh perspective of her pain as we labored together. Her hard work helped her to see that the heart of her depression was in the way she was thinking. Sometimes she would say that she "made a mountain out of a molehill."

Naomi is a very private person. Reaching out for support has been difficult. But she bought into the idea that the Trauma DJ gives you bad advice. When you do the opposite of that inner tape of brokenness, your healing begins. When the Trauma DJ whispered in her ear, "Don't talk about what you are going through; keep people out of your business," Naomi learned to be defiant and reach out for support instead. Learning how to talk her pain out rather than hold it in has really made the difference in her healing. Naomi is no longer depressed, and she no longer takes medication for depression. (Please note that although Naomi discontinued her use of medication successfully, medication management should be done in consultation with your physician. And remember, Naomi is a physician.)

Psalm 23 is a glorious affirmation that because of our relationship with God, there is no need to worry about what our enemies will do to us. We do not have to be fearful of the evil that others plan on inflicting. Nor do we have to endlessly grieve the pain we have experienced at the hands of others. There comes a time when we can settle the old account of pain through our faith. We can learn to thrive, just like Naomi.

PRAYING THE SCRIPTURES

A powerful way to connect with God in prayer is to pray the Scriptures. Think of His Word as a special diet you need to regain your strength. The following key verses from Psalm 23 are in the first person to help you to engage in conversation with God. As you pray through the list, add at least one way each of these promises is true for you.

⮷ You are my Shepherd.

⮷ You give me everything I need.

⮷ You renew my strength.

⮷ Even when I walk through the darkest valley, I will not be afraid.

⮷ Your rod and Your staff protect and comfort me.

⮷ You prepare a feast for me in the presence of my enemies.

⮑My cup overflows with blessings.

⮑Surely Your goodness and unfailing love will pursue me all the days of my life.

Let's Pray Together

Dear Lord, You are my Shepherd. You supply all my needs. Your love is all the guarantee I need. With Your love I can face any pain, any challenge, and any test. I receive Your message, and I no longer fear my trauma. I am not intimidated by evil. I rest in You. I am supported by You. I am strengthened by You. And because of You I can live my life boldly. Give my hands work to do, Lord. I live for You! Amen.

NOW THAT WE HAVE ADDRESSED THE TRAUMA STATION OF "CAN'T COPE WITH YOUR EMOTIONS," WE ARE READY TO FIND THE EXIT SIGNS FOR THE NEXT ASPECT OF TRAUMA, "CAN'T TELL TIME." FOR THOSE WHO LIVE UNDER THE SHADOW OF THEIR TRAUMA, TIME SEEMS TO EVAPORATE. EVENTS THAT HAPPENED YEARS AGO SEEM AS THOUGH THEY ARE PRESENTLY REOCCURRING. BUT AS YOU DEVELOP THE SKILLS TO STAY FOCUSED ON THE PRESENT, THE POWER OF THOSE PAINFUL MEMORIES WILL FADE.

part THREE

Can't Tell Time

The grip of emotional pain is so powerful that it can make time stand still. Memories of pain you went through long ago can be so vivid it seems as though it happened yesterday. It is as if someone put you in a time machine and sent you speeding back to your past misery. Your mind, functioning as a first-rate time machine, causes you to relive every aspect of your trauma. But there's good news. The flashbacks, nightmares, and intrusive thoughts you experience are actually gifts in disguise to help you heal as you learn to make sense out of them. Let's start with the time machine.

chapter 10

The Time **MACHINE**

JUST IMAGINE WHAT YOU COULD DO if sci-fi was reality and time machines actually existed. Anytime you were uncertain about how an important relationship or project would turn out, all you would have to do is jump into your own personal time machine, and *w-h-i-s-k*, you'd be there scoping out your future life. You could see how things would turn out, and if you didn't like it, you would just make different choices to sculpt the outcome you want. How cool would that be?

Time machines could come in handy for past mistakes too. You could just jump in and *w-h-i-s-k*, return to the "scene of the crime." With different words, different actions, voilà; your problem would be solved. Whew, that feels good. Sci-fi is powerful stuff. Fun to think about.

Of course, this is a very old idea. Every generation seems to come up with a time machine adventure. H. G. Wells wrote about it in 1895. In the 1980s, the movie *Back to the Future* featured a zany professor and his young protégé who experienced the thrills of time travel.

Most of us, at one time or another, wonder what it would be like to travel through time. We struggle with wanting to go back to the past, particularly our own past, because of the pain of our guilt. If the technology were really available, who wouldn't jump into a time machine and erase their biggest mistake for starters? Think about it. What would you change if you could go back in time?

If the technology were really available, who wouldn't jump into a time machine and erase their biggest mistake for starters?

And while we're being honest, our anxieties about the future would compel us to take a sneak peek. It's only human nature to want to climb into a time machine and march across the years, zigzagging between the past and the future.

The Bible has its version of time travel. Remember the story of the conversation between Elijah, Moses, and Jesus on the Mount of Transfiguration? They all lived hundreds of years apart, yet Jesus miraculously spoke to them as contemporaries (ca. A.D. 31). Read Mark's report of this miracle of time and space:

Six days later Jesus took Peter, James, and John, and led them up a high mountain to be alone. As the men watched, Jesus' appearance was transformed, and his clothes became dazzling white, far whiter than any earthly bleach could ever make them. Then Elijah and Moses appeared and began talking with Jesus.

Peter exclaimed, "Rabbi, it's wonderful for us to be here! Let's make three shelters as memorials—

one for you, one for Moses, and one for Elijah."
He said this because he didn't really know what
else to say, for they were all terrified.
Then a cloud overshadowed them, and a voice from
the cloud said, "This is my dearly loved Son.
Listen to him."

—Mark 9:2–7

Obviously Peter was overwhelmed by what he saw. But who wouldn't be? Peter had just witnessed time travel. More importantly, it showed Jesus in a completely different light. Jesus rarely revealed His divinity to His disciples. When He did display His power, it was almost always to heal the sick, provide food for the hungry, or bring a message of hope for the despairing. But on this occasion, Jesus showed how ageless, exalted, and utterly breathtaking He and His message are. As the Father said on the Mount of Transfiguration, "This is my dearly loved Son. Listen to him." This same Jesus wrestled with trauma and won, and so can we. Let's learn how.

Trauma makes time collapse.

Jesus, the time traveler, talked to Moses and Elijah in a completely natural and comfortable way. No one knows what they discussed. But we do know that what happens on the "mountaintop" affects how we live in the "valley" where we dwell every day.

From biblical times to the present, time travel remains a source of keen interest. What is mere fantasy for sci-fi enthusiasts is an everyday occurrence for the human mind. When you have survived emotional trauma, you know all too well how your mind can, in a single leap, go back and grab a memory of a troublesome event that occurred perhaps decades ago. The mind can make it seem as though the disturbing episode is happening again right now. Trauma makes time collapse. The normal rules of time appear to be suspended. There you are, reliving an event that happened long ago that you would much rather forget.

Just ask Tina, who was referred to our office by her physician because of a stroke. Her doctor felt that her stroke was brought on by the accumulated stress of traumatic childhood experiences she never addressed. Her physician was right. Tina had so many traumatic memories stored up inside of her it's a miracle that she didn't burst years earlier. Some of the most powerful memories were of events that erupted in her life when she was just about six, some fifty years earlier. As she described her pain, it was clear that her mind didn't experience her horror as a fifty-year-old snapshot. Her mind wrapped this memory up in living color, where the sights, sounds, smells, and textures of the event were so real it was as though it were happening right then.

There were times when the struggle of working through childhood abuse seemed so unmanageable that she thought of quitting her therapy several times. But, in the end, Tina stuck with the process of confronting the time machine in her mind and mastered her trauma. Today she is emotionally and physically fit and thriving personally and professionally. She has learned the power of living life in the present. I joked with her and called her the poster child for emotional/spiritual recovery.

I am convinced that a big part of Tina's progress was learning that trauma truly "can't tell time." A phrase we often used in sessions was "then was then and now is now." When Tina learned to stay grounded in the present, she was no longer the victim of her own thoughts that had the power to transform her mind into a chamber of horrors. Her mind was now freed up to become fertile ground for her creativity that was just waiting to be awakened and used in the service of the Master.

ACTION STEPS ⋎

1. **Stay grounded in the present.** Emotional trauma can sometimes overwhelm you. If you've not already done so, get an experienced support person to help you handle this phase.

2. **Remember that memories can't pose a current threat.** Only dangerous people can. (If you are currently being threatened in any way, that is a whole different issue that may need to be handled with legal/law enforcement professionals.)

3. **Look at a clock and say to yourself the time, date, and location of where you are right now.** This is a helpful way of keeping you from drifting off into overpowering memories. Remember that your mind is a time machine that can go in any direction. It can go back to a painful event or it can move forward to the future.

4. **Keep a journal of your progress.** As you reflect on the memories, think of them as an unfortunate natural disaster that had an impact but now is over.

5. **Most importantly, remember that you are not alone.** God is with you to comfort and guide you through this challenge.

Let's Pray Together

Dear Lord, in Your hands my greatest fears can become a building ground for faith. Thank You for newfound strength that helps me to reclaim myself—body, mind, and soul. Thank You for giving me a mind that is sound and can rebound from hurts and disappointments. A sound mind that chooses to pray rather than worry, that chooses to stand firm in Your grace rather than tremble in the presence of troublesome memories. Today I choose to live in the present and walk in the wonderful power of Your love that keeps me safe. Amen.

NOW THAT WE HAVE ESTABLISHED THAT OUR MINDS TRANSFORM OUR MEMORIES INTO A TIME MACHINE, THE NEXT CHAPTER FOCUSES ON HOW TRAUMA USES FLASHBACKS TO RELIVE THE EVENTS WE WOULD RATHER IGNORE.

chapter 11

The Flashback **MONSTER**

YOU'RE RIGHT THERE, on the edge of your seat. Heart pounding. Forehead sweating. Chest pulsating. Fears mounting. You can see what happened to you. You relive every moment of your trauma, frame by frame. You see it painstakingly, in s-l-o-w motion. You would do just about anything *not* to remember. But you do. You remember much more than you want. Moving these memories out of your mind is like forklifting a mountain.

Trauma can't tell time. That's what makes this aspect of healing from past hurts so unnerving. I call it the "Three-Headed Monster": flashbacks, nightmares, and intrusive thoughts. All three seem to put your current life on hold, whipping you into an emotional frenzy by zapping you into the mind's custom-made "time machine" that takes you back to a place of heart-stopping pain.

Let's talk about the first "head"—flashbacks.

The Bible tells us we are fearfully and wonderfully made. Listen to how the psalmist describes God's creation:

*You made all the delicate, inner parts of my body and
knit me together in my mother's womb.*

*Thank you for making me so wonderfully complex!
Your workmanship is marvelous—how well I know it.*

*You watched me as I was being formed
in utter seclusion, as I was woven together
in the dark of the womb.*

—Psalm 139:13–15

Clearly we were made by God. He created our bodies and our minds with an intricate blueprint. This is good to know, because our suffering often convinces us that we are an accident. On the contrary, this Scripture affirms that we are not an accident, but a divine "on purpose."

Scripture affirms that we are not an accident, but a divine "on purpose."

Your mind in particular was created in such a way that when it is overwhelmed, it can function much like instant replay. In a sporting event, if a play is controversial, the replay cameras will show the play in question from every available angle. Something similar happens with flashbacks.

When you have an emotional experience that overwhelms you, the mind can use flashbacks to help you repeatedly look at something from different angles to see if you can master it through further examination. But what happens, as the scenes replay in your mind, is not a sense of mastery but a sick feeling in your gut that leaves you with a gnawing sensation that you are trapped in a time warp with no way out. Think of it as your unconscious mind's effort to create an instant replay of your trauma.

Flashbacks are intense memories that can surface in various ways such as the following:

- **Image**—a scene from an upsetting memory

- **Smell**—a scent that triggers a traumatic memory

- **Touch**—physical, violent, or sexual contact that evokes powerful memories (Your muscles actually remember certain kinds of touches that were upsetting.)

- **Taste**—that brings back a larger memory of a traumatic event

- **Sound**—auditory trigger that causes you to recall a disturbing scene

- **Feelings**—emotional reactions that evoke memories of the upsetting event

- **Numbness**—absence or dulling of your feelings

When a flashback comes, remember that you have an answer. Your wondrously made mind is talking to you in its own "007" coded language by telling you that it is ready to start looking at what happened to you and make sense out of it. Just like the replay that looks at that close play in sports, the flashback is reviewing your pain so that you can get a healthy grip on what transpired. In a strange way, your flashbacks are an attempt to help you exit *The Trauma Zone* by facing your pain. So go with it.

It is important to process the information in the flashback. This is the best way to

One of the best ways to take the charge out of your memories is to get grounded.

master it. However, it is important to proceed at a comfortable pace. Traumatic memories, especially flashbacks, are extremely powerful; but you can take your power back. One of the best ways to take the charge out of your memories is to get grounded.

In order to work safely with electric power, it is essential to ground the current. Working with emotionally charged memories is similar. Emotional grounding is connecting with the present in a way that feels comfortable and safe. When you feel safe in the moment, you can find the courage to process the flashbacks, remembering that they are just memories now. So, if your mind brings it up, you can look at the memories and not panic because you realize they can't hurt you.

In an excellent article on the subject (http://www.mental-health-matters.com/articles/article.php?%20artID=154), "Coping with Flashbacks: Goals and Techniques for Handling the Memories," Sean Bennick, Vice President of Get Mental Help, Inc., describes a three-pronged approach to coping with flashbacks:

1. **Accept the flashback.** (Allow your mind to recall and understand the traumatic event.)

2. **Control the flashback.** (Interrupt the memory and replace it with comforting thoughts to calm the stressfulness of the memories.)

3. **Escape the flashback.** (Postpone when you deal with the memory. This can be done if the flashback is still too overwhelming.)

Just remember that the flashback will continue until you master its content. Keep at it until you take back your memories. You can take the power from your flashbacks. With God's help and hard work you can do it.

ACTION STEPS

1. **Heal your spirit.** Remember the purpose of a flashback is to heal your spirit from an event that overwhelmed you.

2. **Relax your mind.** Consider flashbacks as an instant replay, not a horror movie.

3. **Process your memory.** Reflect on what you can learn from what happened. Think of it in terms of the measures you need to take to move forward that will keep you safe and help you to move beyond the experience that upset you.

Let's Pray Together

Father, You have taught me that I am fearfully and wonderfully made. You created me to be healthy in body, mind, and spirit. When I have a flashback, it is Your way of saying, "My child, it's time to put these memories to rest." So, I will ground myself in the safety of Your love and face the memories that once tormented me, knowing that as long as I am connected with Your strong arm, I don't have to fear anything—not evil, flashbacks, or enemies.

Thank You, Lord, for sending Your comforting presence. You empower me to face anything, whether it is outside of me or inside my own mind. The replay in my own mind is inviting me to reflect on my painful memories so that I can make sense out of them. I take that invitation today. I am safe in Your love and I am at peace. Amen.

NOW THAT WE HAVE LOOKED AT HOW
THE FIRST HEAD OF THE MONSTER JUMPS
IN A TIME MACHINE AND TAKES US BACK
VIA FLASHBACKS TO MEMORIES WE'D
RATHER FORGET, LET'S FACE THE SECOND
HEAD—NIGHTMARES.

The Nightmare **MONSTER**

TOSSING AND TURNING. Shifting from one side of the bed to the other. Waking up in a cold sweat. The silence of your slumber interrupted by the sound of your own screams. You feel restless and drained the next day because you know you're not getting enough sleep—and the culprit? It's those wretched nightmares!

Emotional trauma is such a formidable foe. Sometimes it seems to chase you, even in your sleep. When your conscious mind shuts off the pain from past hurts, the unconscious mind says, "Thank you very much; I'll take it from here." It replays in your sleep scenes of troublesome memories you naturally prefer to avoid.

The good news is that you can learn from your dreams. Although it's hard to believe that nightmares are a gift, they really are. Nightmares suggest that you are ready to bring to the surface a problem you have been avoiding. When you face the nightmare and wrestle with the painful memories that trouble you most, you will overcome them.

The biblical patriarch Jacob, whose name was later changed

to Israel, was quite a fighter. One of Jacob's best-documented battles was against what many feel was an angel. Let's listen in:

> *During the night Jacob got up and took his two wives,*
> *his two servant wives, and his eleven sons and crossed*
> *the Jabbok River with them. After taking them to the*
> *other side, he sent over all his possessions.*
>
> *This left Jacob all alone in the camp, and a man came*
> *and wrestled with him until the dawn began to break.*
> *When the man saw that he would not win the match,*
> *he touched Jacob's hip and wrenched it*
> *out of its socket. Then the man said,*
> *"Let me go, for the dawn is breaking!"*
>
> *But Jacob said, "I will not let you go*
> *unless you bless me."*
>
> *"What is your name?" the man asked.*
>
> *He replied, "Jacob."*
>
> *"Your name will no longer be Jacob,"*
> *the man told him. "From now on you will be*
> *called Israel, because you have fought with God*
> *and with men and have won."*
>
> *"Please tell me your name," Jacob said.*
>
> *"Why do you want to know my name?"*
> *the man replied. Then he blessed Jacob there.*
>
> *Jacob named the place Peniel (which means "face of*
> *God"), for he said, "I have seen God face to face,*
> *yet my life has been spared."*
>
> —Genesis 32:22–30

This Scripture is powerful. It teaches us that just like Jacob we can get our blessing if we are willing to persevere and wrestle with the issues that previously overwhelmed us. Jacob's name change represents a change of character.

Trauma victims also need some changes to happen so they can move from victim to survivor. That's where our mental time machine steps in to help. It uses nightmares to replay traumatic events to help us master them.

Just like Jacob we can get our blessing if we are willing to persevere and wrestle with the issues that previously overwhelmed us.

There are different categories of nightmares and some universal themes that generally speak to some deep-seated fears we harbor inside. For example:

- A person falling may suggest the need for support we feel we are not receiving.

- Taking an exam but not being prepared may suggest some area of our lives where we feel insecure and need better preparation.

- Fighting with a person or animal may suggest that there are issues we have been battling that need to be resolved.

- Being chased may suggest that there are important issues or people that we need to face.

- Driving out of control and not being able to brake may suggest that there are areas in our lives that appear to be out of control. We would benefit from relaxing and finding a more balanced approach so that we can "enjoy the ride."

• Running stuck in slow motion and being unable to yell may suggest that we are stuck in some area of our life and need to speak out and give our concerns a voice.[1]

Which ones most resemble your nightmares?

Regardless of the form your nightmares take, they have the impact of keeping past pain alive by downloading it into your dreams. Nightmares are difficult to master because they generate so much fear, but what you need to remember is that nightmares are dreams. They can't harm you. Dreams are messages from the unconscious to your waking self. Think of your nightmares as memos from your unconscious that if properly decoded can give you excellent advice on handling a problem that has previously gotten the best of you.

Just ask Shaneekua, who lost her father to cancer. Her grief reaction was very intense. She had many things she wanted to say to her dad. When he died, Shaneekua turned her pent-up anger and frustration inward. She couldn't find the words to express her pain while she was awake, so her agony surfaced through her dreams. She had recurring nightmares of wild animals chasing and attacking her.

Remember, dreams cannot hurt you.

She was referred to therapy by a professional mentor. In treatment, we focused on the issues about her dad that she was unwilling to face. Since her nightmares were the centerpiece of her trauma, we gave considerable attention to this aspect of her care.

Shaneekua made a turning point when I asked her to keep a journal about her dreams and what they meant. I requested

1. The Dream Foundation has a very interesting site that summarizes universal aspects of dreams. See www.dreams.ca/interpretation.htm.

that she write a happy ending to the dreams and keep close to her at night the messages she learned from the dreams. Within a few weeks, the nightmares stopped!

Every survivor's nightmare story is different, but the principle for bringing peace to those nightmares is remarkably similar. Remember, dreams cannot hurt you. They are ideas, wrapped up in a dramatic story that plays in your mind while you are asleep. The key is to understand and decipher those messages. When you can do this, you stop being afraid of your dreams and use them as a springboard for your progress. Sweet dreams!

ACTION STEPS

1. **Reflect on what valuable lessons can be gleaned from the nightmare.** How has God provided for you in your situation? In what ways is God trying to shape your character?

2. **Script a new ending to your nightmare.** Before you go to bed, write down what message you think your unconscious mind is trying to get across to you.

3. **Keep a dream journal and note how your dreams start to shift as you reflect on their deeper meaning.**

4. **Remember to thank God for the improvement in your sleep.**

Let's Pray Together

Dear Lord, with Your help I know I can face my nightmares. I understand that in the grand scheme of things my nightmares have a message for me that I need to master. I need to learn not to be overwhelmed by my fears. I need to learn that if I run from my fears they will only hunt me down in my sleep.

Your Word teaches me that You have not given me a spirit of fear. So grant me, Lord, a spirit of boldness that will allow me to face my fears wherever they choose to pop up. Thank You for the assurance that as my fears lose their grip on my life, I will find restful sleep. Amen.

NOW THAT YOU KNOW HOW TO CONQUER THE NIGHTMARE MONSTER, YOU ARE READY TO TACKLE THE THIRD HEAD OF THE MONSTER—INTRUSIVE THOUGHTS. THIS IS THE ASPECT OF TRAUMA THAT INSERTS TROUBLING THOUGHTS INTO YOUR MIND WHEN YOU LEAST EXPECT IT.

chapter 13

The **MONSTER** of
Intrusive Thoughts

THE LAST OF THE THREE-HEADED Monster is intrusive thoughts. Sometimes, when your life has been "through the wringer," your thoughts start to develop a mind of their own as a way of making sense out of the pain. Unwanted thoughts pop into your mind like popcorn in the microwave right before you slide a good movie into the DVD player. Imagine that each kernel of popcorn symbolizes one of your deepest fears. There is so much popcorn it breaks open the popcorn bag, fills up your microwave oven, and pushes the door open. That's what intrusive thoughts are like—utterly overwhelming.

What makes the intrusive thoughts that pop into your mind so stressful is both their volume and content. They are also huge distractions that keep you on-the-edge and make you ill at ease. Intrusive thoughts invade your mind and "change the station" to their favorite channel—*The Trauma Station*. Rather than focusing on the task at hand in the here and now, those pesky intrusive thoughts refocus your attention to past hurts and cause you to reexperience the pain.

Most often these unwelcome intrusive thoughts bring something to your consciousness that horrifies and offends you. A textbook example of intrusive thoughts was offered by a close colleague who experienced childhood trauma. She confided that at times when she is engaged in a professional dialogue with someone, her mind involuntarily shifts to thoughts of the abuse she endured as a child. All the while she has to maintain her composure and continue an intelligent dialogue. Torture.

Intrusive thoughts invade your mind and "change the station" to their favorite channel— The Trauma Station.

Beyond being painful and stressful, intrusive thoughts are upsetting because they may plant in your mind ideas of harming a loved one, acting out in rage, or imagining you are being inappropriate with someone sexually. Without the proper intervention, these intrusive thoughts gain momentum and can eventually take over your thinking like an avalanche cascading down a mountainside.

The biblical account of Jesus' temptations in the wilderness gives an interesting view of how intrusive thoughts function.

Then Jesus was led by the Spirit into the wilderness to be tempted there by the devil. For forty days and forty nights he fasted and became very hungry.
During that time the devil came and said to him, "If you are the Son of God, tell these stones to become loaves of bread."
But Jesus told him, "No! The Scriptures say, 'People

*do not live by bread alone, but by every word that
comes from the mouth of God.'"*

*Then the devil took him to the holy city, Jerusalem, to
the highest point of the Temple, and said, "If you are
the Son of God, jump off! For the Scriptures say, 'He
will order his angels to protect you.
And they will hold you up with their hands
so you won't even hurt your foot on a stone.'"*

*Jesus responded, "The Scriptures also say,
'You must not test the Lord your God.'"*

*Next the devil took him to the peak of a very high
mountain and showed him the kingdoms of the world
and all their glory. "I will give it all to you," he said,
"if you will kneel down and worship me."*

*"Get out of here, Satan," Jesus told him.
"For the Scriptures say, 'You must worship
the Lord your God and serve only him.'"*

*Then the devil went away,
and angels came and took care of Jesus.*

—Matthew 4:1–11

In preparation for His ministry, Jesus entered into a period of prayer and fasting. The Devil, much like the Trauma DJ, intruded on Jesus' thoughts to distract Him from His mission. Like the Trauma DJ, the Devil was persistent. He kept hounding Jesus about the opportunities for sin, but Jesus redirected him every time. The thoughts increased in their intensity. But Jesus unpacked the Devil's power by rejecting his agenda and replacing it with God's.

When intrusive thoughts invade the landscape of your mind, you can choose to be like Jesus and redirect your thoughts toward reassuring and comforting ones. You can reject the Trauma DJ's definition of the problem and redefine it on your own terms.

The number one challenge when facing intrusive thoughts is the enormous shame people feel about the ideas that flood their minds. They feel guilty and often panic that something is wrong with them for even thinking the thoughts that are invading their minds.

Jesus forced the Devil to back up by countering the intrusive thoughts with the words of Scripture.

When the Devil attacked Jesus in the wilderness, Jesus forced the Devil to back up by countering the intrusive thoughts with the words of Scripture. We can do the same. When our minds are attacked with upsetting thoughts, we can regroup with affirmations from Scripture. We can remember that these unwanted thoughts are an expression of our hurt. As we resolve these old wounds, the intrusive thoughts will lose their strength and gradually wither away.

Just ask Milo, a brave ten-year-old boy who suffered through terrifying intrusive thoughts in the aftermath of 9/11. When he heard the reports of parents being killed in those buildings in New York City and never again seeing their children, he was horrified. He began to obsess that his mother would suddenly die and he would never see her again. He became so afraid that she would die before the day was out, even though she was in excellent health, that for four years he insisted that she come to school every day during lunchtime so he could see her. She had to remain in plain sight the entire lunch period. Only when the lunch recess was over could she return to work. This was extremely demanding on his mother, who was a real estate agent with a full schedule.

In eight sessions of hard work Milo became completely free

from his intrusive thoughts. He was able to heal when he believed that the thought that his mother would suddenly die was not reasonable. Increasingly, Milo was able to recognize that his mother was young and in excellent health. He was able to shift his thinking to recognize that it was the Trauma DJ whispering in his ear, "You've got to see your mom every day because it could be the last time you ever see her alive."

In therapy, Milo was able to learn that panic is a useless emotion. He tapped into another voice inside of him that was calm and reassuring. This voice told him, "It's time to stop worrying about mom. You don't have to ask her to leave her work to check in on you because you're a big boy now." When Milo learned to trust that inner voice of calm, he got better quickly. When we finished treatment, we celebrated his recovery with sparkling apple cider. If only I had thought of bringing some popcorn too, it would have been a perfect ending for Milo's remarkable healing from intrusive thoughts.

ACTION STEPS

1. **Do unwanted thoughts pop into your mind like hot, fresh popcorn?** If your answer is yes, say out loud, "There is hope."

2. **Remember, intrusive thoughts are like ice cubes.** If they don't have the right environment, they will melt. Since intrusive thoughts need an environment of fear to thrive, create an environment of love and faith in your mind instead. For example, Milo believed for years that his mother was going to die at any time. But when he believed that she was going to be fine, his fears lost their strength and dried up.

3. **When an unwanted thought comes to your mind, try not to be shocked or offended.** Instead, just remember that intrusive thoughts are part of trauma's Three-Headed Monster. The undesirable thoughts are an aspect of your trauma that is merely trying to grab your attention and let you know that you are in a lot of pain. The medicine for this pain is a good dose of healthy thinking. So, when those undesirable thoughts come in, just tell them that you understand why they popped up. They are there to remind you, in their cleverly disguised fashion, of how you need to respond: with confidence and clarity that the intrusive thoughts were sent to help you work through your pain.

4. **Meditate on this Scripture whenever an intrusive thought comes to you:**

> *And now, dear brothers and sisters, one final thing. Fix your thoughts on what is true, and honorable, and right, and pure, and lovely, and admirable. Think about things that are excellent and worthy of praise.*—PHILIPPIANS 4:8

Let's Pray Together

Lord, You know that sometimes I worry a lot. You know that sometimes the strangest thoughts pop into my head. They're frightening and upsetting. Please help me to replace destructive thoughts with ones that bring me peace. Help me to reflect on Your goodness rather than imagining everything that could possibly go wrong. Keep my mind and my heart from needless worry.

I acknowledge You as the source of my healing. Only You, Lord, can make me whole. Only You can give me the power to resist the temptation to worry my way through a problem rather than to pray my way through it. Please help me to place my deepest fears in Your strong hands and to allow You to transform my mind into a place of peace and joy. Amen.

NOW THAT WE HAVE LOOKED AT THE DESTRUCTIVE POWER OF LIVING IN THE PAST VIA THE THREE-HEADED MONSTER OF FLASHBACKS, NIGHTMARES, AND INTRUSIVE THOUGHTS, WE ARE READY TO LEAVE THE TIME MACHINE BEHIND AND STEP AWAY FROM THE PAST AND INTO THE HEALING POWER OF THE PRESENT.

Summary of **HOPE—**
The Power of the Now

WHEN YOU ARE OVERWHELMED by bad memories, you may find yourself spinning downward into an emotional nosedive of nightmares, flashbacks, and unwanted thoughts. Your mind, functioning as a first-rate time machine, may make events that happened decades ago feel like they happened just minutes ago as it replays your heartbreaks, disappointments, and tears.

As you recover from trauma, however, you will increasingly gain confidence that you can recapture the vibrancy of your life. Rather than scratching your head in disbelief, you will know what to do because you have discovered the secret.

Trauma operates similar to the battery in your cell phone. If you don't recharge the battery, it loses all of its power very quickly. Much of the power of trauma is in reliving past hurts. But when you learn to shift the focus away from the calamities of the past to the many gifts that are available in the present, you'll be on the pathway to healing and restoration. Remaining connected and grounded to the here and now will insulate you from any power left over from yesterday's tears. Scripture addresses this issue head-on in Matthew 6:31–34:

> "So don't worry about these things, saying,
> 'What will we eat? What will we drink?
> What will we wear?' These things dominate the
> thoughts of unbelievers, but your heavenly Father
> already knows all your needs. Seek the Kingdom
> of God above all else, and live righteously,
> and he will give you everything you need.
>
> "So don't worry about tomorrow,
> for tomorrow will bring its own worries.
> Today's trouble is enough for today."

It's good to know that the ever-consistent Savior is changeless. That's real security!

Living in the present is liberating because it welcomes you to settle old issues and hurts. Trauma can't tell time but recovery can. And the time that recovery uses is now. Living in the now is calming because it helps you to become a sorting expert. You sort out the pain that comes from staying too long in the time machine of your mind replaying flashbacks, nightmares, and intrusive thoughts. You also learn that some emotions are useless just as worrying about the future is useless.

Trauma can't tell time but recovery can.

Let's do a little test. Think of all the times you worried about a problem. How many times did you come up with? One hundred times? One thousand times? Now, of all the times that you worried about something, how often did your worrying change the situation? (Drum roll.) My guess is that your answer would be the same as mine, "Never!" In the same way, worrying about the future won't change it either.

Living powerfully in the present is an entirely different issue. When you surrender yourself to the work that God has assigned you to do right here and now, you create a whole new and exciting future. When you live in the past, your present is full of regrets. You endlessly cry over the "spilled milk" in your life. When you live in the future, your present becomes saturated with worries and fears.

Of all the times that you worried about something, how often did your worrying change the situation?

Living in the past robs you of the opportunities that are available to you right now. It is also likely to be depressing. The past is gone, literally. And because the past is gone, you are powerless to influence it. Similarly, the future is slippery. It's not here yet. You can think and fret about the future, but it is always out of your grasp. Like the past, you can't live in the future either.

When you spend too much emotional energy living in the past or the future, you find yourself in a strange no-man's land between the "already gone" and the "not yet." That state of limbo is a very tough place in which to function and set down roots emotionally and spiritually.

With God's help you can break free from trauma's time machine and its endless reminders of pain and brokenness. Living in the now jump-starts a whole new reality that helps you embrace your true self, one that is powerful and wise.

When you live in the present, you move away from the old patterns of thinking and doing that tied you to your past hurts. Living in the now helps you to focus all the energy that is inside of you for the work that is before you. When you can focus like this, your faith becomes so strong you can move mountains. And the most important mountain any of us are asked to move is to change ourselves. With God's help, learning to live in the now enables us to be transformed from the inside out, one step at a time!

Let's Pray Together

Dear Lord, I acknowledge that I have had a rough time reliving past hurts. There have been moments when my cup has run over with grief. My pain has at times overtaken me. But I remember that You have taught me that I can move on. With Your help I can heal, I can grow, I can detach from the disappointments of the past. I choose to receive Your caring instruction and live in the present. You are my source. I thank You, Lord, for hearing this prayer. Amen.

NOW THAT YOU HAVE EQUIPPED YOURSELF WITH THE TOOLS FOR LIVING POWERFULLY IN THE NOW, YOU ARE READY TO WORK ON THE NEXT TRAUMA STATION, "CAN'T MOVE." PEOPLE IN THIS TRAUMA STATION OFTEN FEEL EMOTIONALLY PARALYZED. BUT AS SOMEONE HAS SAID, "FEELINGS ARE NOT FACTS." LET'S LOOK AT HOW OTHERS HAVE BROKEN FREE AND HOW YOU CAN BREAK FREE TOO!

part FOUR

Can't Move

This trauma station speaks to the different ways that traumatic experiences apply Crazy Glue to the bottom of your shoes. The result—you can't move! When you are overwhelmed with pain, many times it feels as if you just can't go on, so you shut down. At other times, there is so much self-doubt and emotional clutter that weighs on you that progress is difficult to achieve. Procrastination can also derail your growth. The key to breaking the shackles in this trauma station is following through. Let's start our journey through the "Can't Move" trauma station as we highlight how being stuck in neutral is a big part of the picture for many of us.

chapter 15

Stuck in **NEUTRAL**

LIKE A DEER CAUGHT in the headlights of an SUV, emotional pain can be so intense that you freeze. In the "Can't Move" trauma station, lack of life progress is the order of the day. You find yourself starting and stopping projects that are important to you. All too often you feel stuck, sometimes for years, with problems that never seem to totally get resolved. The stagnation you experience has a way of infecting different areas of your life; relationships and careers often suffer as a result.

It's not that you lack motivation. You are putting in the effort to advance, but somehow you always find yourself running in place. You try to step forward, but your feet never seem to be able to shake free from the quicksand that has you in its grip. And you discover that you are sinking when you want to be soaring.

The biblical example of God's people wandering in the wilderness for forty years is an excellent illustration of how trauma and stagnation join hands. The Hebrews were gloriously liberated from the oppressive Egyptian Pharaoh Rameses

II. God's people had been enslaved for centuries, so once they were set free they were so accustomed to being slaves and thinking like slaves that they remained stuck in a backward mind-set that got them into trouble with God. Let's listen in:

> *The Lord was angry with Israel and made them*
> *wander in the wilderness for forty years until the en-*
> *tire generation that sinned in the Lord's sight had*
> *died. But here you are, a brood of sinners,*
> *doing exactly the same thing!*
> *You are making the Lord even angrier with Israel.*
>
> —Numbers 32:13–14

In the same way there was a relationship between the Hebrews' overwhelming stress and their being stuck in the wilderness for forty years (biblical language for "a long time"), so it is with current-day trauma survivors who become mired in their own "wilderness."

Emotional trauma breaks you down in a way that is very personal. It overwhelms you with a fierceness that buckles you at the knees. In this trauma station you have an extremely difficult time making good life choices. It feels as if you are in an emotional fog. You really do feel that you are in a wilderness of the heart.

Do you remember the last time you were really lost? Perhaps you thought you knew where you were going, but in the end you were hopelessly lost. To your dismay you discovered that you had been going in circles after you came across the same landmark five times. Traveling in your own personal wilderness is much the same way. It may seem as though you are making progress until you come to terms with the painful truth that you haven't gone anywhere. You've set goals, but they remain out of reach. You're moving, but you're going in circles.

The experience of becoming immobilized by your trauma often happens in several critical ways:

- **It can stymie important relationships.** Problems tend not to find resolution. Instead, they plummet like an anchor to the bottom of the sea. Conflicts take on a circular quality, waxing hot, then cold, in a dizzying seesaw of pain and confusion. "She loves me. She loves me not . . ."

- **It can make your career become stagnant.** All too frequently, keeping your career on track becomes a very difficult thing to do for people who have gone through trauma. One reason is that trauma creates such an assault on your sense of self that it's easy to forget who you are, what you love to do, and how you envision doing what you love on a daily basis. Instead, in the avalanche of your pain, your focus shifts radically. The main thing becomes surviving. Getting through the day can become the order of the day. When your focus is so intent on just surviving, it's no wonder that you don't have the energy to consistently push your career forward.

- **It can alienate you from your God.** When you turn away from God, you stop growing spiritually. The apostle Paul said, "Let your roots grow down into him, and let your lives be built on him. Then your faith will grow strong in the truth you were taught, and you will overflow with thankfulness" (Colossians 2:7).

God's love for us is not dependent on circumstances.

But we all know that there are circumstances that erupt so severely that we are tempted to doubt God. Imagine for a second if you lived in New Orleans during the fall of 2005 when Hurricane Katrina practically washed New Orleans off the map; or if you lived in Thailand in the aftermath of the tsunami of 2004. The incredible loss of life and property would have tested the very limits of your faith. The trauma of these natural disasters could make you wonder out loud if God still loves you.

We become spiritually bankrupt when we lose our fellowship with Him.

If you allow it, traumatic experiences can invite you to doubt the Savior's love. But the gift of well-grounded faith enables you to stand even when the world around you is shaking.

Horrible things happen to us. Sometimes these calamities ride in on the tidal waves of natural disasters. At other times, emotional earthquakes come as the result of thoughtless human deeds. Either way, we are challenged to rest in the confident assurance that God's love for us is not dependent on circumstances. He doesn't love us more when good things carry us on the wings of prosperity and health. And He doesn't love us less when we have tragic mishaps.

God's love is steady. His love is unchanged by any circumstance. His passion for us cannot be dampened by any storm. His love is truly unconditional. But if we choose to disconnect from His love, our progress will stop in its tracks.

We become spiritually bankrupt when we lose our fellowship with Him. Whether we acknowledge Him or not, God is the source of everything good. If we cut ourselves off from Him, we are cut off from our source and become a mere shell of our true self. Until we allow the Lord His proper place at the center of our lives, we'll just be going through the motions of living.

Trauma can stunt your growth. But the good news is there

is a way out. Just ask Rochelle, a sixteen-year-old high school student who lives on the West Coast. She was normally an outgoing girl—active in the community and school. She modeled. She acted. She played basketball for her school. But lately she had lost interest in activities that she loved the most. She was hibernating and her insightful mother knew it. Mom brought her in for some intensive work during a summer break.

Rochelle was suffering from depression and for good reason. One of her closest friends was raped and murdered. She and her friend were the same age. They had been buddies ever since elementary school. They even modeled together. When her friend was killed, she felt guilty. She wondered why she lived and why her friend died. And she blamed herself for her friend's death despite the fact that there was absolutely nothing she could have done to prevent her friend's murder.

Nightmares interrupted Rochelle's sleep and intrusive thoughts disrupted her during the day. As a result, she had a hard time concentrating and her academic work suffered. In therapy, we rolled up our sleeves and attacked those feelings of survivor's guilt that were stealing her joy. We worked hard together to help her let go of the belief that she contributed to her friend's death.

When Rochelle was able to detach from her guilt that fueled her nightmares and intrusive thoughts, her healing journey took a dramatic turn for the better. Her academics improved. She resumed her interest in sports. And her overall outlook became upbeat. She took control over how she was going to remember her friend. She told me that when she gets married, if she has a daughter, she will name her after her friend. We looked at each other and smiled. Now that's what I call moving forward.

ACTION STEPS ▾

1. **Take time to pray and meditate daily.** This will help you develop a sense of clarity and focus.

2. **Set some goals.** From the quiet place you are developing, set at least one goal for each area of your life:

   ↪Personal

   ↪Professional

   ↪Emotional

   ↪Spiritual

3. **Follow through on your goals.** Remember: one of the core issues that people who are in the "Can't Move" trauma station struggle with a lack of follow-through. But you can buck the trend. Follow through with one important aspect of your goals today.

4. **Celebrate after you follow through.** Congratulations, you have begun your exit from the "Can't Move" trauma station.

Let's Pray Together

Dear Lord, there are times when the force of my pain causes me to be stuck in neutral. When I'm in this place, I am so inundated with worry that I have a hard time getting anything to move ahead. My career, my relationships, and even my relationship with You seem to come to a screeching halt. In times like these, help me to keep my eyes on You. If I turn toward You in the time of trouble, I know that I'll regain my strength. So lead me with Your powerful hand, and I will stand up and move forward in Your grace. Amen.

NOW THAT WE HAVE BEGUN TO IDENTIFY
HOW TRAUMA CAN CAUSE US TO REMAIN
STUCK FOR YEARS, LET'S CONTINUE THIS
DISCUSSION AS WE EXPLORE ANOTHER
ASPECT OF "CAN'T MOVE"—HOW
TRAUMA WEIGHS ON US SO MUCH
THAT WE SHUT DOWN.

chapter 16

Shut **DOWN**

CIRCUIT BREAKERS ARE WIRED into most electrical systems as a matter of safety. The circuit breakers shut the electrical system down if it becomes overloaded or misdirected. This is designed to prevent electrical accidents including shocks, electrocutions, and fires that might result if electricity escapes rather than staying in the wire where it belongs. The shut-down process happens automatically, in the blink of an eye, if the circuit breaker senses that something is amiss with the electrical current.

Emotional trauma functions in much the same way. If your mind senses that you are being exposed to too much pain, a common way that you get through the day is by shutting down. It's one of the creative ways the mind puts a "circuit breaker" on trauma. So, when the pain keeps expanding, you learn to shut it down and detach from people. Trusting people to come through for you becomes risky because the thought of being let down one more time seems unbearable. Instead, you take cover. You disconnect. You isolate. You stop communicating with family, friends, and co-workers. You pull the sheets over your head and put up the Do Not Disturb sign.

Shutdown is the natural reaction to your personal systems being overloaded. The Bible lifts up some compelling accounts of heroes from the Old and New Testaments who were so filled to capacity that they shut down. The most famous shutdown story comes to us regarding the physical death on the cross of our Savior, Jesus.

Shutdown is the natural reaction to your personal systems being overloaded.

The best evidence about the death of Jesus is that He died of trauma. The flogging that He endured, combined with the crown of thorns thrust into His head, being forced to carry the cross, and having His feet and hands hammered to the cross, created such excruciating pain that it was too much for Jesus' human frame to endure. The pain that Jesus experienced on our behalf pushed Him beyond His physical limits. He literally died as a result of shock to His body.

Jesus died more quickly than most people on a cross did. Usually death on a cross was slow. The body typically succumbed to exhaustion. After the victim's legs could no longer hold him up, he suffocated. If a person was particularly strong, the Romans would break his legs to speed up the process. When the Romans came to Jesus, they didn't have to break His legs because He had already died. Jesus' death was different in that the extreme beatings inflicted upon Him sped up His body going into complete shock.

Let's listen to a portion of Mark's account of the mocking and crucifixion of Jesus the Christ:

The leading priests and teachers of religious law also mocked Jesus. "He saved others," they scoffed, "but he can't save himself! Let this Messiah, this King of Israel, come down from the cross so we can see it and believe him!" Even the men who were crucified with Jesus ridiculed him.

At noon, darkness fell across the whole land until three o'clock. Then at three o'clock Jesus called out with a loud voice, "Eloi, Eloi, lema sabachthani?" which means "My God, my God, why have you abandoned me?"

Some of the bystanders misunderstood and thought he was calling for the prophet Elijah. One of them ran and filled a sponge with sour wine, holding it up to him on a reed stick so he could drink. "Wait!" he said. "Let's see whether Elijah comes to take him down!"

Then Jesus uttered another loud cry and breathed his last.

—Mark 15:31–37

What was remarkable about Jesus' suffering and subsequent shutdown was that it was an act of radical obedience to the Father's direction to lay down His life. He did it willingly, even though He was not at all excited about the idea of being "beat to a pulp" and being hung on a cross. In a documentary about Jesus' death, the History Channel said that He was history's most famous torture victim.

What many people don't fully grasp is the degree to which Jesus also suffered emotional and spiritual anguish. Crucifixions were specifically designed to humiliate the victims. Often the person would be stripped naked and left on the cross for days after they had died as an example to would-be detractors of the Roman government of what would happen if they disobeyed Roman law.

Jesus had to be in excruciating emotional pain knowing that none of His disciples were willing to make a stand for Him or even to raise their voices in protest for the unfair way that He was being treated.

Jesus was not just suffering for the sake of suffering.

It was bad enough that Jesus' friends rejected Him. But at some point on the cross, as Jesus bore the sins of the world on His shoulders, He truly felt that God had forsaken Him. And that was just too much to bear—Jesus' body shut down. The physical, emotional, and spiritual trauma was just too much. And the Master breathed His last.

Jesus was not just suffering for the sake of suffering. The prize of Calvary was forgiveness of sin for all humanity. While the cruel deeds on the part of others might bring us to the point where we shut down and throw up our hands, Jesus gives us hope that we can rebound from our trauma and face our challenges.

The pileup effect of broken dreams, lost hopes, and misplaced direction may at times cause you to pull the switch and turn off the lights. But the good news is that with God's help, you can learn to trust again. You can find the strength to try. You can pull the covers off of your head, get out of the bed, and face the world.

Just ask Mary Elizabeth. She lost her husband in a car accident. He died suddenly. They had five children and were happy together. They were planning to go on a vacation. And suddenly, just like that (snap your fingers), she was a single parent. It seemed so unfair. Mary Elizabeth began to question everything. She wondered out loud why God would take her husband from her when she had been what she thought was a good Christian.

Mary Elizabeth began to sink into a deep depression. She stopped attending church regularly. She stopped returning the calls of her closest friends. But when she would go for days without talking, her big sister, Margie, brought her in for therapy.

The work was slow at first. We had to do some good theology work to address the "Why do bad things happen to good people?" question. The answer, of course, is that being "good" doesn't guarantee or entitle us to a storehouse of blessings without any pain or tragedy. What we worked through together is that unavoidable heartaches and setbacks are woven into the fabric of life. The key is to sidestep the preventable calamities and weather the inevitable heartaches without shutting down. Mary Elizabeth discovered that shutting down was a choice that she could opt out of as she learned to tap into her internal resources God had already tucked inside of her heart.

ACTION STEPS

1. **Identify the ways in which you shut down.**

2. **When you feel like shutting down, remember that there are resources you have yet to tap into (see below), and that you are not alone.**

3. **Meditate on these encouraging Scriptures:**

> *He gives power to the weak and strength to the powerless. Even youths will become weak and tired, and young men will fall in exhaustion. But those who trust in the Lord will find new strength. They will soar high on wings like eagles. They will run and not grow weary. They will walk and not faint.*—ISAIAH 40:29–31

That is what the Scriptures mean when they say, "No eye has seen, no ear has heard, and no mind has imagined what God has prepared for those who love him."—1 CORINTHIANS 2:9

Let's Pray Together

Dear Lord, thank You for Your sacrifice of love—a love that was so connected to my need for salvation that You allowed Yourself to be humiliated and broken for me. You willingly laid down Your life for my sake. Teach me, O merciful Lord, to find the strength not to shut down when I feel like pulling the sheets over my head and withdrawing from the world. Help me to discover an internal reservoir of strength to overcome the challenges I need to face today. Amen.

NOW THAT WE HAVE TOUCHED ON HOW TRAUMA CAN MAKE US WANT TO SHUT DOWN, LET'S CONTINUE OUR JOURNEY IN THE "CAN'T MOVE" TRAUMA STATION AS WE HIGHLIGHT ANOTHER ISSUE THAT HINDERS PROGRESS—THE TENDENCY OF TRAUMA SURVIVORS TO BECOME TORTURED BY SELF-DOUBTS.

Tortured by **SELF-DOUBTS**

ONE OF THE MOST POWERFUL things we can ever do with our lives is to choose what we really want. The heart of being formed in the image of God is that as humans we get to exercise free will. As God's children we get to pick which direction our lives will go—toward the brilliance of the light or toward the abyss that is the darkness. The damage that many forms of emotional trauma leave is that choice is preempted and is snatched away from us.

The experience of going through emotional trauma changes all of this. Trauma often leaves you with gaping holes in your self-confidence. You start questioning: "What is wrong with me that I had to go through this ordeal? Was I singled out? Why me?" Hard times can stir up profound self-doubts and fears.

All of us have plenty of times when we doubt ourselves. But when you've danced with trauma, the doubts come more frequently. Unlike drops of water from a leaky faucet, the doubts become more intense like a current tumbling over a waterfall after a torrential downpour.

When your doubts outweigh your beliefs, your life direction

and momentum suffers. You become stagnant. Your life feels stuck in neutral, seemingly forever. Over time your confidence is affected. For some trauma survivors, the confidence gap becomes clear through choice avoidance. For many, making decisions is downright painful. Stating what you want becomes frightful. Choosing is powerful business. People who have lived through their share of trauma often don't feel comfortable making tough choices. You find yourself on an emotional seesaw, where choices have the feel of a moving target you just can't seem to hit. You reason: "Why make a choice when I can play it safe and remain noncommittal for as long as I can?" You straddle the fence. This way you can keep everybody happy, so it would seem.

By exposing his doubts rather than hiding them, he was able to get the help he needed from the Lord.

But self-doubt does not need to be an albatross worn around your neck. It can be a starting point in a continuum of growth, like a mustard seed. Jesus handled a request for help from a worried father who had some gaps in his faith. Let's take a look together at how Jesus handled the reality of self-doubts:

When they returned to the other disciples, they saw a large crowd surrounding them, and some teachers of religious law were arguing with them. When the crowd saw Jesus, they were overwhelmed with awe, and they ran to greet him.

"What is all this arguing about?" Jesus asked.

One of the men in the crowd spoke up and said,

"Teacher, I brought my son so you could heal him. He is possessed by an evil spirit that won't let him talk. And whenever this spirit seizes him, it throws him violently to the ground. Then he foams at the mouth and grinds his teeth and becomes rigid. So I asked your disciples to cast out the evil spirit, but they couldn't do it."

Jesus said to them, "You faithless people! How long must I be with you? How long must I put up with you? Bring the boy to me."

So they brought the boy. But when the evil spirit saw Jesus, it threw the child into a violent convulsion, and he fell to the ground, writhing and foaming at the mouth.

"How long has this been happening?" Jesus asked the boy's father.

He replied, "Since he was a little boy. The spirit often throws him into the fire or into water, trying to kill him. Have mercy on us and help us, if you can."

"What do you mean, 'If I can'?" Jesus asked. "Anything is possible if a person believes."

The father instantly cried out, "I do believe, but help me overcome my unbelief!"

—Mark 9:14–24

The point that Jesus makes here is that anything is possible to a person who has true faith in God. What is fascinating about this passage is that it is particularly welcoming for people whose confidence and faith have some cracks in it. The father in this story is like so many of us. He had some doubts. But Jesus responded to his being honest and transparent. By exposing his doubts rather than hiding them, he was able to get the help he needed from the Lord. The worried father's reply is quite famous. "Lord, I believe; help thou my unbelief" is how the King James Version renders it.

Jesus was always a fan of sincere faith. The Lord invites us to come to Him as we are. We won't be perfect when we approach Him. Perfection is not an option for us earthlings. But what God does expect from us is to be willing followers. If we are open to His instructions, miracles of healing and recovery await us. Working through the snare that is trauma is much the same way.

Faith is the hook upon which God hangs our blessings. Faith is a difference-maker when it comes to recovery

Willingness to heal plays a big part in bouncing back from disappointment. When you've been beat down, put down, and shut down, confidence is often in short supply. You become so saturated with doubts that it becomes hard to move forward.

Your sense of self is one of the chief dimensions of your personality that becomes wounded in severe emotional injuries. Your sense of self organizes your values, preferences, and beliefs. When your sense of self is damaged, your self-esteem is often poor. You become more easily confused about who you are and how to negotiate your wants and needs.

The story of the father with the demon-possessed child was a picture of that very challenge. This father did not know how to get help for his son. He had been asking for help for years, all to no avail. He went to the disciples, but that also proved to be ineffective. So, by the time this dad got to Jesus, he was feeling as though he was at the end of his rope. His reality was that he went to many people for help and no one was able to get the job done for him. He hoped that Jesus could help, but he wasn't quite sure. When a parent is seeking special help for a child and help eludes them for years, they are in *The Trauma Zone.*

But Jesus showed this dad, and He shows us, that if we have even a *little* genuine faith, it is enough. Faith is the hook upon which God hangs our blessings. Faith is a difference-maker when it comes to recovery.

Have you ever wondered what helps a person make the shift from the energy of doubt to the energy of faith? Sometimes it's just a little faith—a spiritual "spark" that lights a fire—that leads you to that first step in the right direction. A step that says, "Even though I've been frustrated with the help I've been getting, if I keep reaching out, I know I'll eventually find someone who *can* help."

It's good to know that Jesus can help. You just have to believe that there is help available for you. This is especially true for emotional hurts. What you believe about your pain can either speed up your recovery or keep you stuck in the "Can't Move" trauma station.

Just ask Frank, a thirty-year-old widower. He lost his wife of ten years, Janine. They were childhood sweethearts and had been together since they were in high school. Losing Janine felt like an emotional earthquake. The foundations of Frank's life were shaken. He had an especially hard time moving on with his life. It took him nearly seven years to let anyone touch Janine's clothes, but he finally let go and allowed her clothes to be donated to Goodwill. But he had doubts about whether there was ever going to be anyone like Janine for him. He became very depressed. He even struggled with ideas of suicide.

The trauma of losing his spouse turned Frank's world upside down. In therapy we focused on addressing his doubts. We started a journey together that helped him to see that overcoming his depression had a lot to do with changing his beliefs about his life and what his future looked like, even without his wife. He came to terms with the reality that we don't get to control the universe. Losses will inevitably come into our lives. But we get to choose how we handle those losses. We can manage them with doubts and fears. Or, like Frank, we can sit with our pain when it comes, reach out for help, and let the love we receive transform us.

ACTION STEPS

1. **Be patient with your doubts and take time to categorize them.**

   ꙮ Make one category of doubts *healthy doubts.* This would be if you have questions about a choice, an activity, or a person and you haven't received sufficient information to make a meaningful decision or commitment. In this case your doubts are serving as a useful screening tool.

   ꙮ Make another category of doubts *issues you need to work through.* Some doubts come as a result of needing to grow more in particular areas. Learning to trust and expect more is a normal part of the healing process.

   ꙮ Make a third category of doubts *those you are not sure are healthy*—growth issues that you need to work through.

2. **Ask your support person for feedback to help you put your doubts in the correct category.**

3. **Accept your doubts as a gift from God.** Mature faith does not fall apart when doubts crop up.

4. Acknowledge that doubts are an essential part of the of recovering from your past hurts.

5. Pray for wisdom and strength to work through your doubts so that you can learn to trust the Lord for an emotional healing—a healing that grounds you in peace and empowers you to move forward.

Let's Pray Together

Dear Lord, my confidence has some holes in it. I know You have all power in Your hands, but sometimes I have a hard time understanding Your omnipotence. I have moments in which I waver and have doubts. Only You know what I've been through. Help me to trust You with all of my heart. Help me to remove the barriers to my growth. Grant me the courage to take action that is nurturing to who I am and who You are calling me to become. I thank You, Lord Jesus, for Your redeeming love that accepts me unconditionally and restores me to wholeness. Amen.

NOW THAT WE HAVE DISCUSSED
THE ISSUE OF BEING TORTURED WITH
SELF-DOUBT, WE CAN EXPLORE ANOTHER
TOPIC THAT KEEPS PEOPLE
FROM MOVING FORWARD—
EMOTIONAL CLUTTER.

Emotional **CLUTTER**

EMOTIONAL CLUTTER LOVES the company of chaos. Sometimes the pain is so great that you need a good distraction. Emotional clutter serves that exact purpose. Emotional clutter lights a fire under multiple issues, typically all at one time. You find yourself speeding from one crisis to another. With too many agendas, you simply cannot focus your energy in any clear direction. With too much pain on your plate, you never really resolve anything. You don't handle problems in depth, so there is no real resolution, no true progress. Instead, you wind up feeling scattered, frayed, and outnumbered by the sheer volume of pressures you have to manage in your life. Does this sound familiar? I thought so.

At other times, emotional trauma feels like you are carrying an elephant on your back. When emotional hurts keep mounting and go unsettled, it can weigh down your spirit so much that your life grinds to a screeching halt. Some people can't move forward because they are so burdened with making other people happy that they forget about themselves. Some people are so filled with self-doubt and self-hatred that it anchors them to their past hurts.

People who have survived the ravages of trauma know what it is like to have their flaws exposed. They feel naked and uncovered. Remember we talked earlier about the meaning of shame. It is an emotion that tells us that something is wrong with us—deep in our core. So, like Adam and Eve, we grab the fig leaves and cover up.

Let's listen to the creation story that highlights how shame first entered the human experience:

Some people can't move forward because they are so burdened with making other people happy that they forget about themselves.

> *So the Lord God caused the man to fall into a deep sleep. While the man slept, the Lord God took out one of the man's ribs and closed up the opening. Then the Lord God made a woman from the rib,*
> *and he brought her to the man.*
>
> *"At last!" the man exclaimed. "This one is bone from my bone, and flesh from my flesh! She will be called 'woman,' because she was taken from 'man.'"*
>
> *This explains why a man leaves his father and mother and is joined to his wife, and the two are united into one.*
>
> *Now the man and his wife were both naked, but they felt no shame.*
>
> —Genesis 2:21–25

When sin intruded on the scene, people began feeling uncomfortable with being who they truly were. So, they covered themselves up. In our original state of unbroken fellowship with God, we were naked and unashamed. We were open, honest, innocent, and at peace with God and each other.

Sin changed our relationships too. First it changed our relationship with God and then with each other. A relationship with God that was open became hidden and strained. The famously romantic declaration in Genesis 2:23, "bone from my bone, and flesh from my flesh," became "It was the woman you gave me who gave me the fruit" (Genesis 3:12). Vulnerability didn't feel natural anymore. Fears, accusations, and strife started to organize the way we related as humans.

Letting go is a consistent problem with anger issues.

The fallout of this contentious way of relating to one another is that our self-esteem suffered greatly. Many trauma survivors talk about living in homes in which they were emotionally abused. They were fed a steady diet of put-downs.

Strange things happen to you when you get stepped on too long. One of the issues that crops up is anger—lots of it. When anger comes in abundance, you develop bad habits like holding on to your frustrations and disappointments.

Scripture teaches us, "Don't sin by letting anger control you. Don't let the sun go down while you are still angry" (Ephesians 4:26). But trauma miseducates us. Trauma teaches us to hold on to resentments and punish people who cross us until they cry "uncle." This is a great strategy for revenge but an awful plan for healing and growth.

This is the simple truth: fighting fairly is a struggle for many trauma survivors because they were treated so unfairly by those who harmed them. So disagreements last much longer than is helpful or biblical. Letting go is a consistent problem with anger issues.

Letting go is also a major concern with guilt burdens. Many Christians firmly believe in the teaching about forgiveness but have real problems accepting forgiveness for themselves. The result is that trauma-bound people are frequently loaded down with feelings of guilt for the mistakes they have made along the way. They can't move forward.

When people pleasing is offered at the altar of your integrity, it has crossed the line and has become too costly.

We all sin. We have all been hurt or have hurt someone else during our journey. We all "stop in our tracks" without forgiveness. We need it. And we thrive on good guidance and encouragement because we were created for edification. So when the opposite happens, it devastates our spirits. People whose souls are saturated in negativity quickly learn self-hatred. They become desperate for approval as a substitute for true self-esteem. Harriet Braiker, in her excellent book on the subject, refers to the dilemma as *The Disease to Please* (New York, NY: McGraw-Hill, 2004).

When people give themselves over to making others happy at the expense of their own joy, they often become "people pleasers." On the surface, people pleasing sounds like a really nice thing to do. But when pleasing others is done at the expense of being who you really are, saying what you truly feel, and doing what you sincerely believe, then people pleasing suddenly becomes toxic. When people pleasing is offered at the altar of your integrity, it has crossed the line and has become too costly. Some of the things that happen to you when you become a people pleaser are:

- Loss of self

- Poor self-esteem

- Resentment

Just ask Jenna, a lifelong recipient of emotional abuse. She shared that she was often criticized and put down by her family. This left her with a gnawing, empty feeling on the inside that nothing she did was ever enough. Jenna would go out of her way for just about everyone in her life to make sure she accommodated their needs in the hope of winning their approval. It was her way of overcompensating for the gap in her spirit left by the hurt of being devalued for years.

So, in our work together, we talked about this aspect of being in the "Can't Move" trauma station. To exit the "Can't Move" station of *The Trauma Zone* you need to do the opposite of what that ol' Trauma DJ wants you to do. And that means to take one step forward—then another. Jenna's step was to give up trying to please the world. She made changes with her family and at work. She still goes out of her way to be helpful, but now she is much better at maintaining healthy boundaries and even saying "no." She just does it with a smile.

She no longer carries the weight of "people pleasing"—always looking over her shoulder with deep pangs of guilt and wondering if she missed an opportunity to make somebody else happy. Now she is guided by the credo that she must love her neighbor, but to love her neighbor as she loves herself.

ACTION STEPS

1. Reflect on the emotional clutter in your life.

➲Are you doing too much?

➲Are you overcommitted?

➲Are you doing things to please others that do not also give you pleasure and fulfillment?

2. Create a "let-go" agenda.

➲What are you holding on to that is preventing your progress?

➲Catch a vision of what your life would be like without those burdens.

➲Talk to other people who have successfully let go of what you are holding on to, and ask them how it felt to let their burdens go.

3. Cluttered lives are complex lives, so:

➲Find ways to simplify your life. Reflect on your core life priorities and do those things first.

➲Focus on nurturing your important relationships. Start with your relationship with the Lord. Then focus on family and friends. These relationships feed your soul.

4. Have fun!

Let's Pray Together

Lord, I've got too many irons in the fire. I'm fighting too many battles today. I surrender. I yield. I am putting every problem I can't handle in Your hands. I know I need to do my part. But there's no need for me to try and do Your job and mine too. Teach me to focus on what I can do. Help me to be resolute about my assignment from You, and give me the strength to carry that out faithfully. This way You will transform my emotional clutter into clarity and my chaos into peace. Help me always to re-member I'm working for You, Lord. Help me no longer shoulder the burden of being a people pleaser. I'd much rather spend my time making sure that You're happy. Amen.

NOW THAT YOU ARE ON THE PATHWAY TO LETTING GO OF EMOTIONAL CLUTTER (THAT KEPT YOU IN A WORRIED FRENZY), YOU ARE READY TO CONQUER THE NEXT CHALLENGE IN THE "CAN'T MOVE" STATION—PROCRASTINATION.

chapter 19

In a **MINUTE**

PROCRASTINATION IS PERILOUS for the survivor of emotional trauma. Time is the one resource that you can't get more of in life. If you lose a job, you can get another one. If you lose a large sum of money in a bad investment, you can make good investments and recoup your loss. But time is a different story. When you waste time, it's gone forever.

Although the problem of procrastination seems like an innocent enough issue, it is actually a major problem to conquer on the pathway of recovery from psychological trauma. That's because it is such an important indicator of healing. Procrastination is another one of those issues that keep you stuck and off the track of your life purpose. People who consistently procrastinate also defer their potential, defray their hopes, and postpone their dreams.

Healing from the quicksand that is procrastination requires an inner fire—a passion for action that drives you forward. You need to get in touch with a higher calling. Have you ever heard someone describe a friend or colleague as being on a "mission"? Well, that's what it takes to break the yoke of procrastination.

Time is the one re-source that you can't get more of in life.

The Bible recounts the fascinating story of Nehemiah, who heard a clear sense of call to rebuild the walls of the holy city, Jerusalem, after they were destroyed by the Babylonians and the Persians. Nehemiah was a devout Jew and a man with a mission.

Let's turn our attention to the work of Nehemiah and use his example to get some practical handles on how to overcome procrastination:

Early the following spring, in the month of Nisan, during the twentieth year of King Artaxerxes' reign, I was serving the king his wine. I had never before appeared sad in his presence. So the king asked me, "Why are you looking so sad? You don't look sick to me. You must be deeply troubled."

Then I was terrified, but I replied, "Long live the king! How can I not be sad? For the city where my ancestors are buried is in ruins, and the gates have been destroyed by fire."

The king asked, "Well, how can I help you?"

With a prayer to the God of heaven, I replied, "If it please the king, and if you are pleased with me, your servant, send me to Judah to rebuild the city where my ancestors are buried."

The king, with the queen sitting beside him, asked, "How long will you be gone? When will you return?" After I told him how long I would be gone, the king agreed to my request.

*I also said to the king, "If it please the king, let me
have letters addressed to the governors of the province
west of the Euphrates River, instructing them to let me
travel safely through their territories on my way to
Judah. And please give me a letter addressed to
Asaph, the manager of the king's forest, instructing
him to give me timber. I will need it to make beams
for the gates of the Temple fortress, for the city walls,
and for a house for myself." And the king granted
these requests, because the gracious
hand of God was on me.*

—Nehemiah 2:1–8

At the heart of Nehemiah's success was his single-minded passion to rebuild the walls of Jerusalem despite opposition. It was traumatic for a devout Jew to see the walls in shambles, but Nehemiah worked through his pain, which was so intense that he openly wept. Clearly Nehemiah was traumatized by the destruction of Jerusalem's walls; but rather than becoming immobilized by his pain, he redirected his angst to his new mission to rebuild the walls. As we follow Nehemiah's journey from start to finish, we get a bird's-eye view of how to overcome procrastination.

In the "Can't Move" trauma station you experience a lack of life progress. One of the clearest ways you can tell if your life has become stagnant is through how well you are doing in the procrastination department.

Some of the core issues at the heart of procrastination are fear of failure and fear of success. In a wonderful book on the issue of procrastination, Dr. Karen Peterson outlines in *The Tomorrow Trap* (Deerfield, Florida: Health Communications, Inc., 1996) how fear holds you in place and pulls you into unproductive patterns of avoiding your life and your healing. Fear of failure results in avoiding key work so that you can't be blamed for your efforts falling short. Many times when you struggle with fear of failure, you function well below your potential. You cover up the fear of failing by not trying. This way the focus is on your lack of effort and not your ability.

You go on procrastinating until you realize that procrastination is a thief.

On the other hand, fear of success results in not wanting to succeed. You fear the extra responsibility and scrutiny that success brings. Success can be quite scary. By inference, with fear of success you are petrified that if people look more closely at you, they will discover that you are a flawed imposter. When you are bound by the fear of success, you consistently sabotage your progress. At the core you don't believe that accomplishment and its responsibilities belong to you. So, to keep the fear of failure and success in check, you continue to put things off. You go on procrastinating until you realize that procrastination is a thief.

Just ask Fela, who works for a government agency. She received one master's degree but went back for a second. All she had to do to receive the second master's was complete her final paper, but three years later the paper was still not done. She was advised that if she didn't go ahead and complete the degree, she might have to start her academic program all over again.

Typical of many people who have suffered through heavy doses of pain, Fela wanted to move ahead with her life but had a very hard time mobilizing herself to act decisively and finish what she started. So, when Fela and I started our work together, we attacked procrastination as an indicator of her life stagnancy.

As gifted as she was, Fela found herself living in fear. She would procrastinate and retreat when she needed to take a position and march forth. But with encouragement and structure, Fela reenrolled in her program, connected with her previous graduate school advisor, and got back on track.

Previously, procrastination was able to sneak up on her because she did not identify it as a part of what caused her to remain stuck. Armed with greater awareness, she recognized procrastination as a critical issue that needed to be addressed. Fela responded to the challenge with fervor. She committed herself to finishing her degree and she did it. A few weeks ago she advised me that she submitted her thesis. She is scheduled to graduate in this academic year. Fela is feeling very good about herself these days. She is planning to launch out as an expert trainer, and she certainly has the credentials to do it now that she has overcome procrastination.

ACTION STEPS

1. **Get in touch with what the Lord has called you to do.** Spend time in regular prayer, asking the Lord to help you tune in to what your marching orders are from Him.

2. **Many times God has already provided powerful clues concerning what He wants you to do.** Those are the things you have zeal for. Follow your enthusiasm and your fruit. "Following your fruit" means that you pay attention to the areas of your life where you have been most productive and effective.

3. **Cultivate passion for the things in life that are important to you.**

Let's Pray Together

Thank You, Lord, for Your strong hand that leads me in the pathways of righteousness. I know that waiting on You is a part of the master plan. I know that waiting on You strengthens my character and helps me to be more patient and consistent and wise. But there is never a time when You need to wait on me.

Help me to put aside the heavy weight of procrastination that causes me to neglect one of my most precious resources—time. I can't ever get one second back. So help me to be a good steward of time. Help me to take action when it is required. This way I can avoid the unnecessary trap of becoming stagnant in my life. Help me to care so much and to cultivate so much passion for what You want me to do, that it becomes increasingly natural to gravitate toward the mission You have set before me. Give me the passion of Nehemiah so that I can rebuild the walls of my life. Amen.

NOW THAT YOU HAVE A HANDLE ON HOW TO OVERCOME PROCRASTINATION, LET'S CONTINUE AS WE WRESTLE WITH ANOTHER ASPECT OF THE "CAN'T MOVE" STATION—THE ISSUE OF SELF-PITY. IT IS A FORM OF FALSE COMFORT THAT MANY OF US RELY ON. LET'S LISTEN IN ON HOW THIS ASPECT OF TRAUMA RAISES ITS VOICE.

chapter 20

Partying with **PITY**

IF THERE IS A TIME AND PLACE for every-
thing under the sun, as it says in Ecclesiastes 3, then certainly
there has to be a time for licking your wounds. When the
brunt of the pain you have experienced goes unheeded and
unheard, you take matters into your own hands and encourage yourself. You tell yourself, "There, there now. It's going
to be all right." You learn all too quickly that the trauma you
experience is often a lonely road. If no one else shows any
empathy, then at least you can show yourself some sympathy.
Some call it self-pity. Others call it a "pity party."

A pity party makes sense if you have been overrun with
stress. And finding empathy and support for your pain has been
like finding a cool spot at noon outdoors in Palm Springs in Au-
gust (a nearly impossible feat). A pity party is better than no
party.

It is popular to tease or razz your family members and
friends when they have pity parties. But when you look at it
through the lens of heartache and hardship, it makes perfect
sense from the perspective of comfort. I have also painfully

observed that when you party with pity too long, you may find that the party never ends. You find that self-pity is at best a temporary fix. You find inevitably that self-pity does not move you forward. If the only pity you get comes from yourself, then you are isolated and disconnected. If you don't get better support, you remain stuck, wear out, and have a difficult time moving forward.

When you party with pity too long, you may find that the party never ends.

Paul, in his letter to the Galatians, addressed this important topic of believers going through extreme challenges and becoming weary of living a godly lifestyle. Let's listen to what Paul says here:

Pay careful attention to your own work, for then you will get the satisfaction of a job well done, and you won't need to compare yourself to anyone else. For we are each responsible for our own conduct.

Those who are taught the word of God should provide for their teachers, sharing all good things with them.

Don't be misled—you cannot mock the justice of God. You will always harvest what you plant. Those who live only to satisfy their own sinful nature will harvest decay and death from that sinful nature. But those who live to please the Spirit will harvest everlasting life from the Spirit. So let's not get tired of doing what is good. At just the right time we will reap a harvest of blessing if we don't give up.

—Galatians 6:4–9

The apostle Paul, in this passage, provides power-packed advice for handling the urge for the battered and bruised to sit back and party with pity. Paul outlines a more excellent way to experience true comfort and release. Paul speaks directly to the hearts of followers who have suffered many trials and tribulations by saying that if we keep our focus, we can take comfort that we reap what we sow.

Spiritual fatigue lies at the heart of partying with pity.

When you are responding to the call God has placed in your life, it is encouraging to know that if we just continue planting good seeds, we will receive the blessings of having a right relationship with Him. A right relationship doesn't mean that everything will be smooth, but a right relationship does mean that we can rest in the assurance that God is pleased with our lives. Just knowing that God is pleased with us can give us a boost that is exponentially more sustaining and uplifting than a pity party.

Paul also says in this passage that we are clearly told to "not get tired of doing what is good. At just the right time we will reap a harvest of blessing if we don't give up" (Galatians 6:9).

Spiritual fatigue lies at the heart of partying with pity. You get tired of waiting on the Lord for help so you provide your own entertainment. You provide your own comfort. But this Scripture teaches us to hang in there and wait for true support— for the help that comes from above. When this help comes, He replaces the pity party with something far more formidable— the peace that passes all understanding described in Philippians 4:7. Seeking this peace can settle you, even in the presence of overwhelming challenges.

Just ask Earline, a worker in the airline industry who recently relocated from the Midwest. She is twenty-eight years old with two children of her own. Her husband left without a fight. He left without an explanation. She woke up, and he was gone. And he left her with his two sons to raise. She has four children to raise by herself.

In the beginning of our work, she went through many stages. She reacted with sadness, with anger, with fear, and at times she understandably responded with bitterness. She was lonely, and she wasn't getting the support she needed. So Earline found herself feeling loads of self-pity. But what we explored together is that her self-pity provided her with no deliverance.

She worked hard to overcome her sense of abandonment. She especially worked to not become bitter. She acknowledged that it was more difficult to raise her family without the emotional and financial contribution of her husband, but she came to believe that self-pity was a useless emotion.

Earline made real progress as she started reaching out to people who could help. She realized that as long as she camped out "in the valley of self-pity," she could not make meaningful progress. She reflected on the passage from Paul that says to "not get tired of doing what is good." In practical terms this meant to continue raising her children. Her husband's boys developed a tremendous attachment to her, and she continued raising and loving them because this is what she believed God was leading her to do. And God replaced her self-pity with His peace.

Earline has been healing by leaps and bounds, and she has promised herself to not look back. The grace with which she handles herself now helps people who come in contact with her. They ask what makes her so strong. They ask her why she is not at all bitter. She just gently smiles and says she doesn't have time to look back in self-pity. She has too much to look forward to now. Being grounded in the promise to not get tired of doing what is good, she will reap her spiritual rewards. She is just waiting for her due season.

ACTION STEPS ⱽ

1. **Be still and sort out how you are feeling.** Think of the times that you had a pity party. Now ask yourself, "How often has self-pity resolved my problem?" Never, right?

2. **Pray for the strength to handle your moments of self-pity differently.**

3. **Anticipate that you will get your "second wind" emotionally when you continue doing the right and loving thing.** Remember, God has promised in His Word to renew your strength.

4. **Consider your fatigue as a badge of honor that comes from working hard at the lifestyle of recovery.**

5. **Look forward to growing and healing as you put these faith steps into practice.**

Let's Pray Together

Dear Lord Jesus, I am so tired of feeling sorry for myself when the going gets rough. I choose instead to acknowledge my feelings, whatever they are. But I also choose not to wallow in my feelings. I will reach out for help from helpful people. I am confident that my needs will be met. I will not always get the outcome I want, but I will adapt to the demands that confront me daily.

Give me the grace to always turn toward You in a time of trouble. Grant me the wisdom to turn my self-pity into self-determination. This way, I will love my way out of my pain. I will choose my way to a better path. Thank You, Lord, for guiding me and for sustaining me today. Amen.

NOW THAT YOU SEE HOW DESTRUCTIVE
IT IS TO ALLOW YOURSELF TO GET
BOGGED DOWN WITH SELF-PITY, PLAN TO
STOP PARTYING WITH PITY. YOU ARE
READY FOR THE NEXT STAGE, TO BREAK
THE SHACKLES AND MOVE FORWARD.

Summary of **HOPE**—
You Can Move Forward

THE POWER OF EMOTIONAL TRAUMA is in its ability to chain you to your past. You want to move forward, but until you learn how to break trauma's hex, you find yourself spellbound—unable to move and unable to grow. You find yourself transfixed, staring endlessly into space, wondering what happened to you. You commiserate endlessly about what "woulda, coulda, shoulda been." You are behind the wheel, but you never take your eyes off the rearview mirror to look at the road ahead of you.

You really want your life to look and feel new; but before you figure it out, your life is strikingly similar to Bill Murray's comedy hit *Groundhog Day*. You feel like the man this film portrays who wakes up and hits the alarm clock only to discover that what he thinks is a new day is really the same day replayed. In many ways, life in the "Can't Move" station of *The Trauma Zone* reminds you of *Groundhog Day*, only it's a tragedy rather than a comedy. It's tragic to become so bound by the wounds inflicted upon you by past pain that you lose sight of the gifts God has placed at your disposal today. It's tragic to get knocked down by circumstances and then to allow being down to become a way of life.

But the good news is that our hurts don't have to have the last word. We can break the shackles of yesterday's tears by trusting God to lead us in a new direction.

It's tragic to become so bound by the wounds inflicted upon you by past pain that you lose sight of the gifts God has placed at your disposal today.

The biblical patriarch, Abraham, became one of Scripture's best examples of allowing the Spirit of God to lead you out of a land of peril into a land of promise. Let's listen to what the writer of Hebrews says about Abraham and where his faith journey took him:

It was by faith that Abraham obeyed when God called him to leave home and go to another land that God would give him as his inheritance. He went without knowing where he was going. And even when he reached the land God promised him, he lived there by faith—for he was like a foreigner, living in tents. And so did Isaac and Jacob, who inherited the same promise. Abraham was confidently looking forward to a city with eternal foundations, a city designed and built by God.

—Hebrews 11:8–10

One of the aspects of your character that break down when there are too many stressful demands on you is that you lose hope and faith that your life can get better. When you lose faith, you lose momentum, vision, and direction. When you lose faith, you become a minimalist. You can only deal with what you can see. But we can break free from the trap of little faith and little hope. We can accept the mantle that our forefather Abraham took on and become free.

Jesus taught us that faith could move mountains.

Abraham had no idea where the Lord was going to lead him. He just knew that trusting God meant he was going to have to break free of the routine he had grown accustomed to following. Abraham understood that he was being called to launch out and explore a land, a people, and a culture he was unfamiliar with.

Emotional healing takes a similar slant. In order to heal from the trauma that embeds itself in your soul and keeps you from moving forward, you need Abraham-like faith to recognize that sometimes healing means you "tear it up and start all over again." In practical terms, it means to be willing to take a careful look at your life and ask, "What is causing me to be stuck right now?" Faith also downloads the courage you need to act on the answer you get from the "Why am I stuck?" question.

Jesus taught us that faith could move mountains. We can speak to our mountains of fear, our mountains of despair, our mountains of broken dreams, and tell them, "Be gone!" It will happen. We can break the shackles that hold us back by changing what we think and expect from our lives. Let's believe together that as we trust in the Lord with all of our hearts, we can make better decisions. It's reasonable to believe that better choices create better outcomes. And better results build up our confidence. With better confidence, we become more comfortable and at peace with ourselves and the work that Christ has called us to do. We become comfortable enough to break free of our shackles and, like Abraham, move forward into a place of divine promise and possibility.

Let's Pray Together

Dear Lord, I have been stuck for a long time. But I'm ready to break free from the shackles of my pain. I allowed myself to be bound by my fears, but I realize that better days lie ahead as I step out on faith. I can be like Abraham and follow You into a better place. I choose to leave behind my past hurts and embrace my new life in You, one day at a time. Amen.

NOW THAT YOU HAVE LEARNED SOME OF THE STEPS NEEDED TO BREAK FREE OF THE EMOTIONAL SHACKLES THAT HAVE STUNTED YOUR GROWTH, YOU ARE READY FOR WHAT LIES AHEAD. THE OPPORTUNITY TO LEARN FROM YOUR MISTAKES HAS THE POTENTIAL TO HELP YOUR HEALING TAKE OFF. LET'S JOURNEY TOGETHER.

part FIVE

Can't Learn

Have you ever been so exhausted cramming for a test that you just couldn't absorb one more drop of knowledge? Suffering through tragedies in your life is much the same. You can reach the point where you become so dazed by your pain that you stop absorbing new information. You stop learning. You repeat the same mistakes and expect different results. When this happens, your trauma is ushering you toward its companion—addiction to substances or processes.

When you are in the "Can't Learn" trauma station, you also struggle with relationships. It feels as if your relationships are a lit fuse and you are on the other end of it.

Let's start this trauma station with a discussion on broken relationships due to trauma. I call it "Trauma Drama."

Trauma **DRAMA**

HEALTHY BOUNDARIES KEEP relationships safe and sane. When boundaries are clear, relationships tend to be stable, predictable, and reliable. You know what your limits are. You know where you stand: you are either on or off, in or out, hot or cold. Trauma-bound relationships are just the opposite. Relationships that have been marinated in trauma are explosive, like nitroglycerin. They are frequently unstable, unpredictable, and unreliable. People who have been through a lot of pain often attract relationships that mirror their own painful path. And more often than not, they tend to cultivate relationships that are loaded with drama.

The upside of dramatic relationships is that they can really sweep you off your feet. If they are nothing else, they are stimulating. The downside of dramatic relationships is that they are so intense, so overwhelming, and so breathtaking that at the end of the day you ask yourself, "What just happened?" The scary part is you usually answer, "I don't know." And that, ladies and gentlemen, is the crux of the problem.

In the "Can't Learn" station of *The Trauma Zone* you find

yourself in relationships that have far more excitement than you need, but you still get caught up in the drama. Here are some key aspects of "trauma drama" relationships:

Relationships that have been marinated in trauma are explosive, like nitroglycerin. They are frequently unstable, unpredictable, and unreliable.

• New relationships take on a whirlwind quality. You go too fast too soon and get deeply involved before you know the person well. You pull back from the relationship and have "buyer's remorse." You may have feelings of guilt and shame.

• Established relationships may have a start and stop quality to them. Communication shuts down or becomes explosive. There are occasions where physical, verbal, and emotional abuse cloud and intensify the picture.

• A third party may enter the picture, which further intensifies the relationship.

• Conflicts tend to be circular. You have the same arguments repeatedly.

• Conflicts tend to continue with no end in sight.

• Conflicts are often avoided.

• Conflicts include "history lessons" with problems from the past frequently brought in to prove a point.

- You have a hard time learning from your mistakes.

- Often one or both partners have a history of emotional trauma.

If these issues sound painfully familiar, you may indeed have a "trauma drama" relationship.

The Bible has many relationships that had way too much drama. The wonderful thing about Scripture is that it is brutally honest about the faults and foibles of the people it describes. Take, for example, the story of Jacob. He was planning to wed Rachel, only to find that Rachel's dad switched brides on him. Let's read an excerpt of that passage together:

So Laban invited everyone in the neighborhood and prepared a wedding feast. But that night, when it was dark, Laban took Leah to Jacob, and he slept with her. (Laban had given Leah a servant, Zilpah, to be her maid.)

But when Jacob woke up in the morning—it was Leah! "What have you done to me?" Jacob raged at Laban. "I worked seven years for Rachel! Why have you tricked me?"

"It's not our custom here to marry off a younger daughter ahead of the firstborn," Laban replied. "But wait until the bridal week is over, then we'll give you Rachel, too—provided you promise to work another seven years for me."

So Jacob agreed to work seven more years. A week after Jacob had married Leah, Laban gave him Rachel, too. (Laban gave Rachel a servant, Bilhah, to be her maid.) So Jacob slept with Rachel, too, and he loved her much more than Leah. He then stayed and worked for Laban the additional seven years.

—Genesis 29:22–30

This passage has all of the ingredients of trauma drama. It has intensity. (Jacob was so enraptured by Rachel that working for seven years to marry her seemed like a day.) The passage has mystery. (Switching the brides definitely adds a secret agent quality to the story.) Jacob waking up and finding that he was married to Leah rather than Rachel adds a comedy/tragedy component to the story. The passage has passion. (Jacob became enraged with the father for misleading him and demanded that he let him marry Rachel.)

The wonderful thing about Scripture is that it is brutally honest about the faults and foibles of the people it describes.

If you were to ask Mario and Bea, the story of Jacob, Rachel, Leah, and Laban sounds too much like their own drama. In fact, when I shared the Jacob story with Mario and Bea, they laughed and said they didn't know that the Bible had so much drama in it. Mario and Bea confided that from their earliest dates they had heated arguments. Bea confessed that she has always had a temper. And when Mario "got on her last nerves," as she put it, she cussed him out.

Not to be outdone, Mario was a perfectionist. He routinely screamed at Bea when something in the house was not to his liking. These arguments were legendary. Neither backed down. They have broken up and reconciled five times in the last three years. When their mutual pastor referred them to me, it hit them like a ton of bricks that their relationship was out of control.

In therapy, we identified that they both came from homes that were verbally and emotionally abusive. They started to see that they were replaying scenes from their own childhood in an eerie, unconscious script.

Solid progress was made as they both committed to eliminating the abuse from their relationship. They stopped yelling at each other. They remembered that overreacting was a sign of trauma. They connected perfectionism with being tied into their shame. Gradually, they began to see that the trauma that had organized their relationship gave them a style of drama that drained them. They started to buy into the idea that recovery from their trauma gave them a balance and a perspective that was fresh and invigorating. I knew they were solidly on the path to wholeness when Mario and Bea started one session with a reflection that the only time they raise their voices now is when they sing in the choir. We all had a good laugh.

ACTION STEPS

1. **Acknowledge where your trauma background has resurfaced in your current relationships.**

2. **Keep track of your contribution to the problem.**

3. **Remember, the only person you can change is you.**

4. **A good starting point is to ask for what you want and need in your important relationships.**

Let's Pray Together

Dear Lord, I must confess I have too much drama in my relationships. Arguments seem to take on a life of their own. Communication is spotty. Fellowship with my loved ones is too often broken. My relationships take on an all-or-nothing quality. Help me today to start on the pathway to settling things down. Give me the wisdom to say the right words. Help me to be more patient with my issues and the challenges of others so that I can learn from my mistakes rather than repeat them. Help me to overcome the problems that have overwhelmed me. Amen.

NOW THAT WE HAVE ENTERED THE
"CAN'T LEARN" TRAUMA STATION WITH
A DISCUSSION OF THE DRAMA IN OUR
LIVES, LET'S CONTINUE WITH HOW AD-
DICTIONS CREATE THEIR OWN UNNECES-
SARY EXCITEMENT. WE'LL BEGIN WITH
ALCOHOLISM. I REFER TO IT AS
"STRANGE BAPTISM."

chapter 23

Strange **BAPTISM**

SOME THINGS JUST GO TOGETHER: black and night, white and snow, sunny and California, heat and sweat, water and wet. Trauma and addictions are another duo. Many recognize how rampant addictions are in our culture. However, few really understand that the raw material from which addictions are woven comes from the fabric of emotional trauma.

Addictions are driven by the pain we harbor deep inside of us. They are our way of trying to find comfort and a magical elixir to heal the gaping wounds in our hearts. Addictions are our way of medicating ourselves, and they're just bad medicine.

There is a powerful connection between emotional trauma and addictions. This connection is based on our need to escape from the pain that torments our souls. When a substance is used to change the way we feel, it becomes addictive. Our emotional trauma generates such intense suffering that we put all of our energy into avoiding the pain. Our unfaced feelings become the breeding ground for addictions. The psalmist put this sentiment to poetry when he said, "Oh, that I had wings like a dove; then I would fly away and rest!" (Psalm 55:6).

Alcoholism is an attempt to seize dovelike wings and escape, only it doesn't work. It is an attempt to drown your sorrows and fill an empty space inside of you with an external solution. Wise people who understand addictions are quick to point out that "recovery is an inside job." Alcoholism, like all other addictions, is a problem of spiritual bankruptcy. People drink, in part, to fill the void in their souls. People drink because they are empty inside; they have lost their purpose and focus. The alcoholic lifestyle chooses life distractions over life direction. The only way to overcome an addiction is through making a total commitment to a lifestyle change that includes connection with new people, places, and things.

> *Alcoholism, like all other addictions, is a problem of spiritual bankruptcy.*

In the lifestyle of recovery, your focus shifts away from drowning your anguish with alcohol to developing a relationship with God that gives you new hope and meaning. Baptism symbolizes a "changing of the guard." This is a life-giving, replenishing force. Baptism represents cleansing from sin. It symbolizes the purifying of your heart and mind in preparation for divine service.

This is exactly what Jesus did at the beginning of His earthly ministry. Before His baptism, His life is a relative mystery although by faith we can affirm that His life was still very purposeful during those years. When He met John in the Jordan River, His baptism signaled the beginning of His earthly ministry. His baptism also affirmed that having a right relationship with God is the center of a lasting transformation. Our relationship with God gives our lives meaning and purpose. Let's listen together to Matthew's account of the baptism of Jesus:

*Then Jesus went from Galilee to the Jordan River to
be baptized by John. But John tried to talk him out of
it. "I am the one who needs to be baptized by you,"
he said, "so why are you coming to me?"*

*But Jesus said, "It should be done,
for we must carry out all that God requires."
So John agreed to baptize him.*

*After his baptism, as Jesus came up out of the water,
the heavens were opened and he saw the Spirit of God
descending like a dove and settling on him.
And a voice from heaven said, "This is my dearly
loved Son, who brings me great joy."*

—Matthew 3:13–17

Jesus' baptism is a wonderful model for personal transformation. His baptism showed that, although sinless, Jesus was not suffering from arrogance. That would have shown up if He refused to follow God's instructions to be baptized. Jesus showed through His baptism that He was willing to ask for help. And that is exactly what the doctor ordered for us sinful humans who struggle with many issues, including alcoholism.

When you turn your life over to God, He offers you a serenity that is mind-boggling.

This passage is extremely relevant for many reasons and especially for people suffering from the disease of alcoholism—a disease of emptiness driven by a shame-based need to drink your way to a solution. No matter how much alcohol you drink, the nagging pain and the hollow void that echoes against the walls of your heart are painful reality checks that there is no lasting peace in a bottle. When you turn your life over to God, He offers you a serenity that is mind-boggling.

Just ask Martin, who grew up in the Germantown section of Philadelphia, Pennsylvania. He shared that he grew up in a family environment where he was exposed to alcoholism on a regular basis. His father made beer in the basement and from an early age, having access to alcoholic beverages was problematic for Martin. He routinely went downstairs to steal some beer and "get a buzz." He even later admitted it was bad-tasting beer.

His grandfather, who lived close by, often excused himself from family gatherings because of a "headache." He then went upstairs to have a drink of sherry. It wasn't long before Martin figured out that his grandfather was an alcoholic.

By the time Martin was fifteen, it became evident that he was also on a collision course with alcoholism. The very first time his parents *allowed* him to drink, he was at a family reunion. He was given some Coke and rum and became intoxicated.

Increasingly, Martin found that he was living his adolescence and young adulthood through a drunken haze. He crashed the family car twice while under the influence. He was undaunted because his parents did not hold him accountable for his out-of-control behavior. Martin also felt he had things under control—he was a gifted college athlete—as long as he was able to perform at a high level the next day.

Like everyone else with any addiction, Martin reached *tolerance*—the condition in an addiction that causes you to need increasing amounts of a substance to achieve a high. There is a saying when a person is suffering from alcoholism: "One drink is too many and one thousand is not enough." Alcoholism created a gaping hole in Martin's soul that no amount of booze could fill.

Martin attended a prestigious Ivy League college, yet he was more interested in drinking than studying. He couldn't keep up with the work or with his life. Eventually he was asked to leave for a period of time because he was so unproductive. He started working odd jobs before he returned to college. Still his alcoholism consumed him. When Martin finally did return to college, he dropped out one semester before graduation.

Martin slipped into a deep depression. His life revolved around getting high. He eventually started adding marijuana to his addictive repertoire. It was fun at first until his marijuana abuse led him into such intense bouts of paranoia that he lived in constant fear of being arrested. He would drink after smoking marijuana to "medicate" the paranoia the "weed" gave him. His life was spinning out of control. His dependence on alcohol and marijuana hijacked his life.

His road to recovery began when he started attending 12-step meetings. Recovery helped him to become aware that he was living in *The Trauma Zone*. His relationships were shallow. His values were hollow. He didn't know how to live. Recovery gave him his life back.

Martin went back to college and finally completed his degree. He now has a maturity and depth to his life that was previously missing. His faith in God has restored him. He has been clean and sober for twenty years. He shows up for his life now. He used to drown his sorrows in alcohol. Now his life exudes positive energy. He is confident and clear that he can learn from his mistakes—that he is a part of the solution.

ACTION STEPS ▾

1. **Ask yourself some tough questions:**

    ➲Do you cover up your feelings with alcohol?

    ➲Has alcohol made your life unmanageable in any way—family, career, health, legal issues?

2. **If alcohol has made your life unmanageable, seek support.** Alcoholics Anonymous meetings in your community are an excellent place to start.

3. **Turn to Jesus and ask Him to give you the strength to start your recovery from alcoholism if that is your challenge.**

Let's Pray Together

Thank You, Lord, that alcoholism doesn't have the last say when we turn our lives over to You. My addiction to alcohol is more powerful than I. But You are stronger than my desire to drown my sorrows in alcohol. Give me the strength to face my pain and to be baptized in Your love and grace. Amen.

NOW THAT WE HAVE DISCUSSED ALCOHOLISM, ANOTHER ISSUE IN THE "CAN'T LEARN" STATION OF *THE TRAUMA ZONE* IS HOW OUR TRAUMA SUMMONS OTHER ADDICTIONS SUCH AS COCAINE AND SEX. WHY? ADDICTIONS ARE GROUPIES. THEY LIKE PLENTY OF COMPANY. WE WILL CALL THIS DISCUSSION "HIJACKED."

chapter 24

Hijacked

AN ADDICTION HIJACKS YOUR LIFE. It doesn't matter how much money you have or how much power or education you have. Addictions do the same thing to all of us. They hold us hostage. With our hands raised and masking tape glued to our mouths, we are rendered powerless by our addiction of choice.

You can tell that you are gripped by an addiction if you consistently turn to any substance (alcohol, marijuana, cocaine, crack, etc.) or process (sex, overeating, work, shopping, etc.) for emotional comfort. When you are hooked, you say things you never would have said before—things you later regret. You do things and afterward shake your head in stunned amazement. With tears streaming down your face in embarrassment, you say to yourself, "I can't believe I really did that."

Under the influence of an addiction, your personality changes. You do things that are thoughtless, careless, and reckless. You literally become a different person. Your values change. Your conversation changes. Your daily routine changes. Your choices change. The real you gets stuffed in a closet. And a stranger, your addiction, starts to run every part of your life. You hunger for it. You crave it. You yearn for it. You worship it. You build your life around it.

> *Living with an addiction is like trying to fill up a bottomless glass.*

But the addiction is never enough. Living with an addiction is like trying to fill up a bottomless glass. You keep pouring, but the glass remains empty. But that doesn't stop you from pouring. With an addiction, you are handcuffed to your twisted passions. You are in *The Trauma Zone*—a place where you don't learn from your mistakes. You keep repeating the same tragic lessons until you die, lose your mind, or get help.

The biblical record provides us with a powerful account of a man who fell on hard times and lost his mind. He was at the end of his rope when he met Jesus. Just in the nick of time he received what he needed from the Master. Let's listen in on how Jesus handled this special situation:

> *Then Jesus demanded, "What is your name?"*
> *And he replied, "My name is Legion, because there are many of us inside this man." Then the evil spirits begged him again and again not to send them to some distant place.*
> *There happened to be a large herd of pigs feeding on the hillside nearby. "Send us into those pigs," the spirits begged. "Let us enter them."*
> *So Jesus gave them permission. The evil spirits came out of the man and entered the pigs, and the entire herd of 2,000 pigs plunged down the steep hillside into the lake and drowned in the water.*
>
> —Mark 5:9–13

Can you imagine having a mental illness so severe that you'd feel more comfortable living in the cemetery than in your own home? That's where this man lived—in the cold, lonely, deafening silence of the graveyard. It must have been overwhelming. Isolation had done strange things to him. Nobody seemed to understand him. He didn't even understand himself. People were afraid of him. He was homeless and friendless. He cut himself. He roamed the mountainside. He screamed a lot. He frightened people.

But he didn't scare Jesus. Rather than becoming intimidated, the Master saw his behavior as a cry for help. Jesus asked what his name was. He said, "My name is Legion, because there are many of us inside this man" (Mark 5:9). There was a lot going on inside of him—literally. His life was fragmented. His resources were limited.

Some problems are so painful and complex it really does feel like you've got to split yourself into a legion of people in order to survive. Jesus spoke directly to the source of his torment, and the story concludes that this formerly naked madman was clothed and in his right mind after his encounter with Jesus.

Many people tell me that when they have loved ones who are struggling with an addiction, the changes to their personality and their lifestyle make it seem like they are possessed by evil. Who could argue? When you've seen sex and cocaine addiction up close, who could deny that these are modern-day "demons" of our culture?

Just ask Cindy, a twenty-five-year-old recovering cocaine, sex, and love addict. She was a child of the big city who was introduced to trauma at an early age. When she was only nine, her uncle approached her for sexual favors every weekend. He would give her $25.00 and booze when they would meet for their secret rendezvous. When she got paid for sex at such an early age, it set the stage for a defining experience.

Derek, the neighborhood pimp masquerading as a father figure, recruited her to become a streetwalker. He reeled her in with sweet words and promises of attention and nurturance. She was an impressionable fifteen-year-old with visions of making it rich on the streets. Within a few weeks of meeting, he sent her to conferences where she was trained by hustlers on how to be a prostitute, write bad checks, and engage in identity theft.

As Cindy began her life as a street-smart hustler, she had a rude awakening. She discovered that the promises of glitter and gold were empty. Derek, who seemed so compassionate initially, showed that he was in reality quite brutal. He routinely abused Cindy. He would punch and kick her with steel-toe boots if she didn't bring in her quota of money, and then he would send her back out to walk the streets until she brought in enough.

Cindy found herself constantly in dangerous situations. She engaged in acts of unspeakable degradation just to survive. She felt desperate and trapped. She was able to stop working for Derek only when a rival pimp challenged him for having his "girls" turn tricks in his territory. The result was that Derek was gunned down and killed.

Cindy continued her life as a "working girl" and kept the money for herself. She eventually got married, but her husband turned out to be a cocaine addict. Before long she was hooked on cocaine as well. She hit an all-time low as a result of her dependence on cocaine. She used while she was pregnant, and her baby boy showed evidence of cocaine in his system. Approximately two years later her children were removed from her care by Children and Youth Services. It was clearly one of the most traumatic experiences of her life; but that's where her addictions took her.

Cindy identified with the man suffering from mental illness in Mark 5. To protect herself from the enormous pain she was experiencing, she learned to numb out through sex and drugs. And like Mark's demon-possessed man, her acting out brought a legion of problems. Not only did she lose her children, she lost many good jobs because she wasn't able to perform when she went to work high. She lost her self-esteem. And she lost hope.

Cindy's life turned around when she began a 12-step program for her addictions. She connected with a sponsor and has a new lease on life since she has given up drugs and alcohol. Her life now has clarity, purpose, and power as she is learning to walk with the Lord.

When Cindy shared some of her story with her pastor, he referred her to the Pastoral Counseling Network. As we began our work, we focused on the trauma she'd experienced, which consistently placed her in harm's way. Cindy also gamely mustered the courage to begin her recovery from sexual addiction. Her life is transforming right before her eyes. Cindy says that she feels as though she has been to hell and back.

If you have an addiction, remember that your addiction doesn't have to have you.

The success she is seeing is helping her to learn from her mistakes and to leave *The Trauma Zone* behind. Cindy's problems were legion, but with her newfound faith she is taking back a life that was hijacked by her addictions—one day at a time.

ACTION STEPS

1. **If you have an addiction, an important first step is to admit that you are having a problem to at least one person you trust.**

2. **You are not alone.** If your trauma has driven you to an addiction, reach out for help.

3. **Twelve-step programs that match your addiction are a good place to begin your road to recovery.** Most addictions have a Web site with the name of the addiction followed by the word "anonymous" and a schedule of regional meeting places.

4. **If you have an addiction, remember that your addiction doesn't have to have you.**

Let's Pray Together

Dear Lord, at times my life feels out of control. I take comfort in knowing that I am not alone. I may have an addiction, but I rejoice that Your unconditional love embraces me regardless of the presence or absence of any problem. There are times when my pain has led me down destructive paths, including addictions. I am grateful that the antidote to any ailment can be found in Your love and grace. So, it is with courage that I choose to face my trauma with the support of Your love and the caring people You are sending into my life. Amen.

BEING A DISCIPLE OF JESUS CHRIST IS ALL ABOUT LEARNING FROM HIM. LET'S PAUSE FOR A MOMENT AND REFLECT ON THE HOW-TO'S FOR EXITING THE TROUBLESOME TRAUMA STATION OF "CAN'T LEARN." I AM CONVINCED THAT "YOU CAN ACHIEVE MASTERY."

Summary of **HOPE**— You Can Achieve Mastery

TRAUMA SURVIVORS TEND TO BE mastered by their stress. They tend to make the same mistakes repeatedly. But with our hand in the Shepherd's hand, we can approach our lives with an open mind and an open heart. We can study and ultimately master the lessons we need to learn to dwell in His peace.

Have you ever watched a dog chase its tail? Round and round it goes, in a speedy blur, to nowhere. Emotional trauma is eerily similar. Your trauma-saturated relationships may become so waterlogged with drama that it feels as if your personal life would provide an Emmy-award-winning script for your favorite soap opera. Or the course of your trauma may have lassoed you to an addiction. Your life may have so many ups and downs it feels like you are in a bull-riding contest, complete with a cowboy hat and hee-haws.

Hope enters the picture when you break the cycle of your trauma by learning from your mistakes. Recovery helps you to figure it out. Circular problems never end. Like the dog chasing its tail, as long as you are in the circle of your pain, you continue to suffer.

Trauma is a rough schoolmaster, but the payoff is hollow. No one could deny that trauma-bound relationships can be exciting. But our tendency to get too close too fast, argue our points too intensely, shut down communications so completely, and follow up on solutions so inconsistently, more often than not leaves us empty-handed and brokenhearted.

The pairing of our pain with our addictions of choice is also a bedeviling dilemma. Between intoxicating substances (smoking, alcohol, marijuana, cocaine) and mind-numbing processes (sex, romance, overeating, gambling, shopping, work), the truth is that our addictions make our lives unmanageable. They simply overpower us and pin us to the floor for a three count, just like in wrestle mania.

Hope enters the picture when you break the cycle of your trauma by learning from your mistakes.

The path of healing is also challenging, but it is richly rewarding. Jesus taught us that the road leading to righteousness is hard; but compared to the burdens of allowing our pain to make us bitter and cause us to stray from God, His burdens are a cakewalk. Let's listen to how the Master teaches this lesson to His disciples:

"Come to me, all of you who are weary and carry
heavy burdens, and I will give you rest.
Take my yoke upon you. Let me teach you,
because I am humble and gentle at heart,
and you will find rest for your souls."

—Matthew 11:28–29

The fascinating aspect of this passage is that the yoke Jesus is speaking about is the burden of wisdom. This wisdom leads you to connecting with the issues that are most important to the Father: loving Him and loving each other. Developing a mature relationship with God takes work. It requires prayer, patience, and a willingness to follow instructions from God's Word. But the fruit far outweighs the burden. And for those of us who struggle with burdens that, like anchors, are tethered to our souls, the ability to download unlimited love, grace, and peace is a real relief.

Developing a mature relationship with God takes work

The companion burden of loving each other is also hard. Loving people is perhaps a bit harder than loving God. God is perfect. People, on the other hand, have attitudes that conjure up loads of stress. We are often short-tempered, unforgiving, and unhelpful. But as we apply Jesus' instructions in this passage and follow His lead, we will find ourselves helping each other even when we're tired, bearing each other's burdens even when we are flirting with exhaustion, and listening with compassion even when we have felt unheard. We can begin to do this because the wisdom of Christ shows us that His love inside of us is replenishing. We give. We become tired. But when we connect with our Savior, He gives us extra strength to continue with our journey.

We can learn from our mistakes, and learning from our errors is powerful. It breaks the cycle that keeps us in our addictions and in relationships that are so strange it seems like we are following an instruction manual overnighted to us from another planet.

Our recovery gives us a whole new lease on life. We start

to realize that we are no longer victims. It also dawns on us that we can alter our choices. We can develop relationships that are healing and mutually satisfying as we commit ourselves to make these relationships work.

We can come out of our addictions.

We can come out of our addictions. One day at a time, we can experience the gift of recovery as we gather the courage to face our pain. We can learn to tap into the uncommon strength that is already lying dormant inside of us, waiting to be called out of darkness and into God's marvelous light. We can master our trauma. How? By learning that regardless of the pain that was imposed upon us and that disfigured our true selves, we can follow the lead of our Christ. We can transform our misfortune into a treasure chest of growth by allowing God's love to override our fears.

ACTION STEPS

1. Meditate on Matthew 11:28–29, the focus Scripture for this chapter.

2. Name three fears you have been worrying about that you can release today.

3. What are the hidden strengths that you are discovering inside of you? List three for starters.

Let's Pray Together

Thank You, Lord, for giving me a way of breaking the cycle of my pain. I am learning, one day at a time, to master my fear with an extra portion of Your love and grace. Amen.

Now that we have discussed the "Can't Learn" station of *The Trauma Zone*, the final trauma station we need to explore is the "Can't See" trauma station. In this station emotions are so intense we become like an ostrich with our heads buried in the sand. We avoid difficult situations because we feel that avoiding our trauma will make our troubles magically disappear. So we deny, ignore, and distance ourselves from our woes. One small problem—the avoidance program doesn't work.

Let's see why.

part SIX

Can't See

This section of The Trauma Zone *highlights the tendency of some survivors to avoid difficult emotions. The more you run from an issue you need to face, the stronger your trauma gets. But when you stand firm and face your pain, it dries up and loses its force.*

Talk to the **HAND**

THE NEXT TIME YOU HAVE an opportunity to visit the zoo, look up the ostrich. Ostriches are the largest bird in the world. They can grow up to nine feet tall and can sprint at a pace of forty miles per hour. Not bad for a bird that can't fly. But ostriches are most famous for something they don't actually do in real life—bury their heads in the sand. If they did that in the wild, they would have become extinct long ago.

When I listen to the many stories of people stuck in the "Can't See" station of *The Trauma Zone*, I think of ostriches burying their heads in the sand to escape their predators. Although this behavior is a myth, it perfectly symbolizes the struggle of many of us in *The Trauma Zone*.

When we are frightened, the most natural thing in the world is to bury our heads in the sand. When trouble is circling our lives as in Custer's Last Stand, we instinctively hide. We duck. We take cover.

One way we hide out from our trauma is to deny our problems. There are many creative ways we make denial happen.

We pretend the problem doesn't exist, minimize the challenge (trivialize major issues), or ignore a problem hoping it will magically disappear.

When we create too much distance between us and our pain, we detach.

You can tell when you are in the "Can't See" station of *The Trauma Zone* when you find yourself habitually avoiding painful concerns. You react with anger at the mere mention of anything on your list of hot "do not talk about these or else" issues. Such topics make you squirm. They make you feel uncomfortable and vulnerable. And you would do just about anything to sidestep feeling exposed.

The consequences of staying in this trauma station are that we become spectators of our own lives. When we create too much distance between us and our pain, we detach. And when we disconnect from the reality of our suffering, we start to drift emotionally. Sometimes our heartache becomes so unmanageable that we forget who we are.

That is exactly what happened to the prophet Elijah. He had some epic battles with the priests of Baal (an ancient god of the Canaanites) on Mt. Carmel in modern-day Haifa. Even though Elijah experienced God's deliverance from the prophets of Baal, he was still intimidated by Queen Jezebel. She sought to execute him for his stance with God. Let's listen to what the biblical record says about the time Elijah became overwhelmed and ran away:

When Ahab got home, he told Jezebel everything Elijah had done, including the way he had killed all the prophets of Baal. So Jezebel sent this message to Elijah: "May the gods strike me

and even kill me if by this time tomorrow
I have not killed you just as you killed them."
Elijah was afraid and fled for his life. He went to
Beersheba, a town in Judah, and he left his servant
there. Then he went on alone into the wilderness,
traveling all day. He sat down under a solitary broom
tree and prayed that he might die. "I have had
enough, Lord," he said. "Take my life, for I am no
better than my ancestors who have already died."

—1 Kings 19:1–4

Despite Elijah's mighty feats against the prophets of Baal, he was "shaking in his boots" when Jezebel went after him. He panicked and got out of town. When he stopped running, he made one of the strangest prayer requests in all of Scripture. He asked God to put a "hit" out on him. Imagine that—a prayer warrior asking God to kill him!

Yet when you understand how trauma works, Elijah's prayer request makes sense. Jezebel's threats of murdering him were more than he felt he could handle. Jezebel traumatized Elijah; and in this state, death seemed more appealing than life.

Like Elijah we too find ourselves in situations of overwhelming stress. When this happens, we find a place to hide. We seek the pseudosolace of denial.

Just ask Billy, a thirty-year-old engineer who is a whiz at work; but before therapy he was petrified of intimacy. Getting him to spend quality time with his family to discuss issues that require emotional vulnerability had the appeal of pulling teeth with pliers.

Billy is working hard in therapy to pick up the inner cues of his fear of closeness that had its roots in his horrific childhood abuse. In his early teens while on his way to run errands, Bill was pulled into an abandoned home and accosted. The individual who attacked him was deranged, and was eventually sent to prison for raping and murdering a woman. The memory of his attack as well as living in a household that was filled with yelling and violence sent Billy reeling into *The Trauma Zone.*

Home was not safe for Billy so he sought sanctuary at work. He quickly became skilled at his engineering tasks and lost himself in his work. His employer and clientele love that he is such a hard worker. But Bonnie, his wife, loathes the time he spends away from the family.

The Trauma Zone is helping Billy to see that the unrest he grew accustomed to in his childhood is over. He no longer has to lose himself in his work. He has a beautiful wife who adores him. He is learning that the emotional distance he used to maintain a semblance of peace is agonizing for Bonnie. He is learning that as long as you run from your fears, they chase you; but when you stand firm and face them, the need for denial dries up. And so does the pain that keeps the fears revved up.

Most of all Billy is learning that in order to live his life, he needs to be fully present. He feels safe today and no longer needs to say to Bonnie (and others who love him) "talk to the hand." Instead, he reaches out his hand and grabs hers.

ACTION STEPS ⋎

1. Read this passage to focus your energy:

"This is my command—be strong and courageous! Do not be afraid or discouraged. For the Lord your God is with you wherever you go."—JOSHUA 1:9

2. Cultivate fear-busting strength by meditating on this powerful Scripture.

3. **Keep an emotional healing journal—this can be a powerful tool in recovery.** Note how applying the principles in this passage encourage you to face your fears.

Let's Pray Together

If it were not for You, Lord, when my pain overwhelms me, I would bury my head in the sand like the ostrich. But when I remember Your mercy and Your grace, I receive new courage. I want to stretch my wings like the eagle. I believe that if I face my problems, You will help me to fix them; but if I run away, they'll never get better. So I stand on Your redeeming love that takes things that are wrong and makes them right. Amen.

AFTER A TRAUMATIC EXPERIENCE SOME PEOPLE FEEL IT IS BETTER TO GO THROUGH LIFE WITH THEIR BLINDERS ON. THE HIDDEN BELIEF OF PEOPLE IN THIS TRAUMA STATION IS THAT "IGNORANCE IS BLISS." CHRONIC AVOIDANCE OF PAINFUL TRUTH IS THE ORDER OF THE DAY. THE DESIRE TO KEEP EVERYONE HAPPY AND NOT ROCK THE BOAT IS A PROMINENT THEME. ONLY IF NECESSARY TRUTH IS IGNORED CAN IT BE PULLED OFF. BUT WHEN THE BLINDERS ARE REMOVED, YOU CAN FACE LIFE ON ITS OWN TERMS. AND WHEN THE TRUTH IS FACED AND INGESTED, IT TRANSFORMS. STAY TUNED.

Ignorance Is **BLISS**—Right?

HAVE YOU EVER HAD A PROBLEM that was so large you said to yourself, "Spare me the details; I'd rather not know"? When pain like this pops you in the head, you don't want to handle more. You want less, much less. You want to limit your burdens. You want to lighten the load. You become a master at avoiding your trauma. The truth feels too intimidating, so you go around it, minimize it, accidentally-on-purpose forget about it, or just plain pretend it doesn't exist.

When your emotional pain is like Mount Everest in its enormity, who could blame you for ignoring the elephant in the room? After all, what's an elephant compared to the mountain of pain you feel you've been climbing forever?

These are mitigating circumstances. Under these conditions, ignoring your anguish is certainly understandable. Yet we know that solutions that are understandable and helpful are two very different things.

Although it is far more convenient to sidestep our trauma with a smooth samba of avoidance, the reality is that dodging our problems never gives us lasting relief. At best our credo of "ignorance is bliss" only offers us a temporary fix for our distress.

Hightailing it from problems doesn't work to settle our woes. In *The Trauma Zone* we know that the more we run from the issues that trip us up, the more we remain the same.

Hightailing it from problems doesn't work to settle our woes.

In contrast, our walk with the Lord teaches us to wrestle with the truth. What emerges from our struggle with reality is that we become stronger. Working through our pain is often what makes us whole as we settle the issues that dogged us.

Jesus understands exactly what we are going through in the "Can't See" station of *The Trauma Zone*. The gospel of John recounts what He taught His disciples about being whole and free. This is what the Master said:

Jesus said to the people who believed in him, "You are truly my disciples if you remain faithful to my teachings. And you will know the truth, and the truth will set you free."

"But we are descendants of Abraham," they said. "We have never been slaves to anyone. What do you mean, 'You will be set free'?"

Jesus replied, "I tell you the truth, everyone who sins is a slave of sin. A slave is not a permanent member of the family, but a son is part of the family forever. So if the Son sets you free, you are truly free."

—John 8:31–36

Jesus is addressing the potent issue of spiritual bondage here. Essentially, when you place anything in your life before God, you become a slave to it. It masters you and represents sin for you. Your sin becomes a spiritual stronghold with such force that only God's Son, Jesus the Christ, can release you from its grip. In this rich passage, Jesus is declaring His authority and credentials to release us from the spiritual strongholds that wreak havoc in our lives.

Essentially, when you place anything in your life before God, you become a slave to it.

Our emotional trauma fits into the category of spiritual strongholds that ushers in so much mayhem that avoidance makes sense—until we connect with the Savior who is greater than any sin problem or stronghold.

In John 16 Jesus again taught His disciples about handling situations in which the odds against us appear overwhelming. He said, "But take heart, because I have overcome the world" (John 16:33). This is good to know.

Jesus overcame the problems of this world and we can too. Although we have traveled down a pathway that has included emotional anguish, we can rejoice that our hard times don't have to chase us forever. We can learn to trust God with all our hearts and face the issues that caused us sleepless nights. Our hurts will lose their power. The more consistently we look our trouble square in the eye, the more something powerful will begin to happen. We get stronger and the trauma gets weaker.

Just ask Consuela. She is quite a charmer. She also is a survivor of trauma, but like most survivors you could never tell by her suave external appearance. Consuela grew up in a home where she was victimized by a combination of physical, emotional, and sexual abuse. Her family life was chaotic and often hostile. Eventually, she was placed into foster care to keep her safe.

Jesus overcame the problems of this world and we can too.

As an adult, Consuela learned to cope with the pain she harbored until it ballooned out of control. She was a successful businesswoman who loved to shop. Her wardrobe was impeccable. Despite her solid income, her compulsive shopping led her to the brink of bankruptcy. When we explored this in therapy, it became clear that her shopping was geared toward filling a void in her life. Through shopping she was buying approval. She hoped that with all of the trappings of success she purchased that she would win the approval and esteem she desired.

Consuela also confided that she hated being alone. She dated people who, in her own words, were "awful matches" for her just to avoid the pain of being alone.

In therapy she is developing a new focus that is liberating. She is learning to detach from trying to win the approval of others through buying their affection. She is also discovering how to love herself and enjoy her own company, and to build a whole new relationship with the Savior. She is now able to affirm the passage from John 8:36: "So if the Son sets you free, you are truly free."

ACTION STEPS

1. **Take a step forward armed with this powerful affirmation:** "My life will be transformed when I face my problems rather than run from them."

2. Memorize this encouraging Scripture:

> *"For I can do everything through Christ, who gives me strength"*—PHILIPPIANS 4:13.

3. Take another step forward with this affirmation: "I am a child of the light. When I am faced with the truth, I ingest it rather than flee from it."

4. Meditate on this Scripture:

> *"You are the light of the world—like a city on a hilltop that cannot be hidden"*—MATTHEW 5:14.

Let's Pray Together

Dear Lord, I have lived in fear when that seemed to make sense. But I am grateful that I can move my life forward recognizing that ignorance is not bliss; it is costly. So, I step out in Your strength. I choose today to build my life around faith and not fear. I choose today not to run from the issues in my life because the light You put inside of me is stronger than the darkness. I will stand on the truth that I am the light of the world. I believe that You have set me free. Amen.

NOW THAT WE ARE EQUIPPED WITH THE
KNOWLEDGE THAT IGNORANCE SETS US
UP FOR FAILURE, WE ARE READY FOR THE
NEXT STEP OF THE "CAN'T SEE" TRAUMA
STATION: "CATCH ME IF YOU CAN."
LET'S PUT ON OUR SNEAKERS!

chapter 28

Catch Me If You **CAN**

WHAT WAS YOUR FAVORITE CARTOON?
Mine was definitely *The Road Runner.* I loved seeing that
skinny bird run circles around Wile E. Coyote. No matter how
hard Wile E. pursued the star of the show, he could not catch
him. The Road Runner was on a mission never to get caught.

When we have been pursued as a result of our own personal
Wile E. Coyotes, like the Road Runner we also learn the art
of the quick escape. We learn how to sense when danger is
breathing down our necks. We've learned the tricks of the trade.
So, when the Trauma DJ signals the alarm deep inside of us that
trouble is on the horizon, we can put on escape moves that
would put the great Houdini to shame.

One way that we keep painful emotions at arm's length is
to not let people get close to us. A great way to get people to
back off is to approach them with a closed mind and a closed
heart. For the short run, the effect of having a closed mind when
you are engaged in a dialogue with someone is incredibly powerful. A closed mind lets the person know you could not care
less about what they think. A closed heart lets the person know

that you could not care less about how they feel. The net result is that you clear the room. People who at one time appeared to pose a threat have become so discouraged in talking with you that they leave you alone. The danger is gone—right? Wrong!

One way that we keep painful emotions at arm's length is to not let people get close to us.

Actually, the doors to our mind and heart (that our Trauma DJ so eagerly closes) are the same doors that help us to gain access to the support we need in order to heal. The closed-door approach to our minds and hearts fosters isolation and is emotionally suffocating.

In order to rebound from our emotional tempests we need tons of support. But our pain, more often than not, makes us suspicious of other people's intentions because of what we've been through. We cut off communication. We become reluctant to reach out for help because we fear that a request for support may be a sign of weakness. Therefore, we pull ourselves up by our bootstraps and suffer in silence.

A wonderful story in the Old Testament about a preacher named Jonah is a powerful reminder of our initial analogy of the Road Runner and Wile E. Coyote. God called Jonah to preach a message of hope to the people at Nineveh, but Jonah initially felt overwhelmed by this assignment. He considered the Ninevites beneath him, so he ran from his divine calling. But God stirred up the ocean and caused the ship to almost break apart and sink. The sailors picked Jonah up and threw him overboard. He was swallowed by what most of us presume was a whale. Listen to a repentant Jonah in the belly of the big fish:

Then Jonah prayed to the Lord his God from inside the fish. He said, "I cried out to the Lord in my great trouble, and he answered me. I called to you from the land of the dead, and Lord, you heard me! You threw me into the ocean depths, and I sank down to the heart of the sea. The mighty waters engulfed me; I was buried beneath your wild and stormy waves. Then I said, 'O Lord, you have driven me from your presence. Yet I will look once more toward your holy Temple.' I sank beneath the waves, and the waters closed over me. Seaweed wrapped itself around my head. I sank down to the very roots of the mountains. I was imprisoned in the earth, whose gates lock shut forever. But you, O Lord my God, snatched me from the jaws of death! As my life was slipping away, I remembered the Lord. And my earnest prayer went out to you in your holy Temple." . . . Then the Lord ordered the fish to spit Jonah out onto the beach.

—Jonah 2:1-7, 10

Jonah loathed the assignment that God gave him. He ran as fast as he could, expecting the worst. This mind-set is identical to the thinking style of trauma survivors. When our lives are stressful, we often expect the worst from people and from outcomes. It is this kind of negative faith that fills our minds and hearts with life-crippling fear.

It took Jonah being swallowed by the darkness inside the fish for him to see the light.

It took Jonah being swallowed by the darkness inside the fish for him to see the light. In the midst of his predicament, he reached out to God. He discovered that it was through his prayer and subsequent willingness to serve the Ninevites that help and deliverance became available. He moved from being inside the whale to dry land. What a relief to obey the call of the Lord!

Many times the Lord asks us to do things that are so difficult we would rather jump off the boat and right into an ocean. The gift of Jonah's story is that as he worked through the fears that literally swallowed him, he discovered uncommon strength to stop running *from* God and to begin running *for* God. Working through the pain of your trauma is quite parallel. The more you believe that running from your troubles sets you up to be lost at sea, strangely adrift from the purpose and high calling that God has for your life, the sooner you can garnish the power to face the "demons" that once tormented you. Victory is then right around the corner.

Just ask Paul, whose story is amazing. As a child, he was neglected by his birth mother. She was an alcoholic who left him and his sister alone for long periods of time. On one occasion when he was about seven years old and his sister was a toddler, he became so hungry that he got on a chair and attempted to make fried chicken for them. Because he was so young and inexperienced, he merely browned the skin of the chicken rather than cooking it through. This is what he was reduced to eating.

He figured out that living with his mother was too unsettling, so he approached his father to see if he could live with him. His dad consented and Paul went to live with his father and stepmother. Little did he know that his father was suffering from major depression. He was often short-tempered and verbally and physically abusive with Paul. Over time, Paul learned to avoid his dad out of fear of criticism. One day, after coming home from high school, he was greeted by police who told him not to go downstairs because his father had just hung himself.

You can only imagine the combined effect that motherly neglect and fatherly abuse had upon Paul's development. In order to cope with the enormous pain that was percolating inside of his heart, Paul learned to be an emotional "distancer." For example, he masked his pain by dating many women while in one primary relationship.

In therapy, he learned some powerful insights. His broken relationship with his mother contributed to him developing a pattern of relating to women in a way that was intense yet superficial. The other insight he learned was that his strained relationship with his father contributed for many years to him not wanting much of a relationship with his heavenly Father. He rarely went to church.

As we worked together, Paul came to terms with his tendency to run away from both God and people. He discovered a newfound faith in the Lord. He surrendered his former pattern of dating other women on the side and is enjoying being faithful to his partner of many years. More importantly, the void that created so much pain and that had him running for his life is now filled with the discovery that he is a son, loved by his heavenly Father.

ACTION STEPS

1. Meditate on Psalm 91:1–6:

Those who live in the shelter of the Most High will find rest in the shadow of the Almighty. This I declare about the Lord: He alone is my refuge, my place of safety; he is my God, and I trust Him. For He will rescue you from every trap and protect you from deadly disease. He will cover you with his feathers. He will shelter you with His wings. His faithful promises are your armor and protection. Do not be afraid of the terrors of the night, nor the arrow that flies in the day. Do not dread the disease that stalks in darkness, nor the disaster that strikes at midday.

2. **Consider how the promises from this passage help you become more confident in facing your fears.**

3. **Using the inspiration of this Scripture, think of one way that you are willing to launch out and face today.**

Let's Pray Together

Dear Lord, when it feels as though I'm being swallowed whole by memories of painful experiences, help me always to remember that I am kept afloat by Your love. There are times when I would rather run and take cover from my pain, but not today. Instead, I choose to find my refuge and comfort in Your loving protection. Amen.

NOW LET'S REFLECT TOGETHER ON
WHAT WE HAVE LEARNED TO HELP US
STAND FIRM AND FACE THE ISSUES
WE WOULD RATHER AVOID.
I CALL IT "SUMMARY OF HOPE—
FROM FEAR TO FAITH."

Summary of HOPE— From Fear to Faith

EMOTIONAL TRAUMA CATAPULTS you into a strange place where you go out of your way to avoid your pain. The Trauma DJ grabs the bullhorn and exhorts you to deny, hide from, ignore, and shut down your mind and heart from anything that reminds you of your fears. The good news is that it can be truly liberating when you understand how trauma works. The more you heed the voice of the Trauma DJ, the more mired in quicksand you become. The more you connect with God's strength deep inside of you, waiting for you to call upon it, the more you are freed to escape from the fears that had you trapped.

Denial is a symptom of our trauma. When we have fears that we can't face, denial rears its ugly head by prompting us to put in the earplugs. In this trauma station, we shut out feedback we don't want to hear. We embrace the credo of "ignorance is bliss." We close our minds and shut down our hearts when we feel intimidated by our distress.

Powerful hope is poured out to us as we embrace the message from Psalm 23:5:

*You prepare a feast for me in the presence of
my enemies. You honor me by anointing my head
with oil. My cup overflows with blessings.*

In this biblical classic, we are encouraged to be still and confident. These instructions are given with the understanding that enemies with hostile intentions are all around us. But instead of feeling panic and dismay, we are exhorted to remain secure because of God's promise. He will anoint our head with oil.

When we have fears that we can't face, denial rears its ugly head by prompting us to put in the earplugs.

The shepherds of ancient Palestine anointed the sheep with oil to help heal their scrapes and wounds. In a similar manner, God, through the power of His Spirit, heals our emotional wounds. He does this with His Word, which changes our beliefs. Our transformed faith helps us to think about our experiences differently. We can see, despite the ill intentions of others, that God has a purpose for us that both precedes and supersedes the harmful designs of our detractors.

In this passage, we can see another powerful promise unfolding right before us. When Scripture says, "My cup overflows with blessings," it affirms God's plan to have us experience abundance in the midst of our challenges. It is intriguing that God's blessings are not offered to us apart from our suffering but rather through our turmoil.

The message is clear and helpful. The Shepherd's love is so powerful that hard times and hard people that place us in impossible situations are no match for the love of God. We do not get to control the universe. Difficulties will come. The missing link, however, which we do have control over is our faith in our God who is more than able to comfort and deliver us from any foe.

Now that you have journeyed through each of the five trauma stations, you are ready to leave *The Trauma Zone* behind. When you get out of *The Trauma Zone*, the gravitational pull to return to the old ways of thinking and responding is formidable. But don't be afraid. God's light is stronger than the darkness you've lived through. In "Continuing on the Transformation Highway" we will discuss how we need to close the door and throw away the key to *The Trauma Zone*. What lies ahead in our transformation is a whole new life strategy that is healing and powerful!

The Shepherd's love is so powerful that hard times and hard people that place us in impossible situations are no match for the love of God.

Continuing **ON** the Transformation Highway

THE NEW TESTAMENT WORD for transformation is the same root word that is used for metamorphosis. Interestingly, one of nature's masterpieces of transformation is the caterpillar as it is going through the miracle of metamorphosis. The caterpillar is one of the least attractive, most pathetic insects in all of creation. It is so lowly, it can't even walk. It crawls on its stomach. But after it goes into its cocoon, it emerges as a butterfly—beautiful and majestic. The caterpillar starts out crawling but ends up with a spectacular set of colorful wings. Now that's what I call transformation!

Something similar happens to us when we leave *The Trauma Zone*. We too have an emotional metamorphosis. Our transformation has three primary characteristics:

- We close the door to our traumatic past.

- We taunt our trauma (face our pain with boldness).

- We develop the courage to thrive.

Let's begin our transformation journey with the notion of closure.

CLOSE THE DOOR AND THROW AWAY THE KEY

Old habits are a bear to break. When you have lived in *The Trauma Zone* for much of your life, it is only natural to respond the way you always responded to your tribulations. When we leave *The Trauma Zone*, there is a tremendous rush. You feel that the gorilla you have been carrying on your back has finally gotten off. The relief is exhilarating. You feel brand new. You become more confident. You feel better about yourself. But you quickly discover that even though you have begun to transform the way you think about your challenges, the world around you has not gone through the same metamorphosis that you have.

It is not our job to control how others choose to manage their lives.

In practical terms, people who were uncaring may still be that way. It is not our job to control how others choose to manage their lives. But we do get to manage our own lives. More specifically, our healing is in our boundaries. Remember, boundaries keep relationships safe and sane. Boundaries help us to be clear about what we accept, want, and need. We never again have to take on someone else's negativity.

We can have setbacks in our healing journey when we encounter people or circumstances that appear unfair and we react with that sick feeling, deep inside of us, that nothing is going to change. The Trauma DJ starts its chant: "Here we go again. Nothing you do is ever going to make a difference. Why did you bother to try to change yourself anyway?"

If we buy into the Trauma DJ's argument, we will end up

back in *The Trauma Zone*. The key is to remember not to fall for the trick of making our role in the scheme of things too grandiose. The only person we can change is ourselves.

We can only be pulled back into *The Trauma Zone* if we handle familiar problems by over-reacting with panic, rage, or despair. If our trauma is all about being overwhelmed, then our recovery is all about looking at each of our challenges and discovering where the hidden blessings are.

The only person we can change is ourselves.

Tucked inside every trial is an opportunity to grow. The words from Joseph's traumatic story, after his brothers sold him into slavery, ring especially true here:

> *"You intended to harm me, but God intended it all for good. He brought me to this position so I could save the lives of many people."*
> —Genesis 50:20

Can you imagine brothers being so filled with rage that they sold one of their own into slavery? But rather than retaliating and harming his brothers for what they did, Joseph behaved like a man on a healing journey. He blessed his brothers and restored the family relationships that had been fragmented by deceit and jealousy.

Like Joseph, we can declare about our heartache, "As far as I am concerned, God turned into good what you meant for harm." By remembering that the old strategies never worked, you take a crucial first step toward staying out of *The Trauma Zone*. Practicing your new coping skills of moderating your feelings (Can't Cope with Your Emotions), living in the present (Can't Tell Time), moving forward one step at a time (Can't

Move), learning from your mistakes (Can't Learn), and facing your fears (Can't See) keep you out of harm's way. You can look at your past hurts, shut the door to your own personal trauma zone, and throw away the key by remembering that regardless of the harm that befalls you, God will work it for good.

TAUNTING OUR TRAUMA

The second stage of transformation is "Taunting Our Trauma." When we move out of *The Trauma Zone*, one important change that occurs in our journey toward wholeness is that we simply stop being intimidated by the pain that once tormented us. Victim behavior ceases. Instead, we learn over time to taunt our trauma. This means that we boldly face our pain, listen attentively to the voice of the Holy Spirit inside of us, and follow the course that God has set before us. Inevitably, the Trauma DJ will bring to our attention some reason why we need to back up, put our tails between our legs, and limp away. But because we have left *The Trauma Zone*, we don't run away. We focus. We pray. We march forward.

We don't let anything deter us. We buy into the vision that the prophet Isaiah shared of a time when God's people would be so in tune with His will that nature itself would change. This is what Isaiah said:

> *In that day the wolf and the lamb will live together;*
> *the leopard will lie down with the baby goat.*
> *The calf and the yearling will be safe with the lion,*
> *and a little child will lead them all.*
>
> —Isaiah 11:6

This passage is powerful good news for those of us who have experienced our share of emotional upheaval. But the radical idea of the predator and the prey lying side by side is not an invitation for us to become our predators' club sandwich. This is a prophetic declaration that God will change us. Even if we are surrounded by evil, we will not be consumed or over-taken by it.

The Trauma DJ gave us a rotten script. We played the role of a panic-driven person whose character ran in circles screaming "help." Our transformation has given us a new script. We walk straight ahead now, with determination and resolve. And when we spot trouble, we slow down and instead say, "What can I do to help?" We are able to help ourselves and to help others because we are on the mend.

Our trauma is like a snowflake.

We are people who have become whole because we have learned the secret. Trauma is no match for us. Our trauma is like a snowflake. As people on the mend, we are like a hot oven. No matter how cold that snowflake is, if it is placed in the hot oven, it's going to melt. Trauma is the same way. Without an environment of worry and fear, our trauma falls apart. When we understand how our trauma works, we can make it fall apart every time as we do the opposite of what the Trauma DJ instructs us to do.

Our trauma has no power over us when we learn to be at peace in the presence of our pain. We recognize dangerous peo-ple and situations, but now we know how to stay out of harm's way. We choose not to go into a frenzy when challenges cross our paths. Instead, we have learned to work through and hur-dle our difficulties. We use our past hurts as fertilizer for our growth. We now have the courage to thrive.

COURAGE TO THRIVE

The opposite of being in *The Trauma Zone* is thriving. It is the last stage of transformation. It begins with the belief that God has intended all along for us to have His best. This doesn't mean that we won't have trials—quite the contrary. But when we align all of the resources in our Father's hands that He imparts to us against the travail we experience on earth, we have more than enough resources to cope. Our cup runs over. We thrive.

Our emotional distress has been a thief.

In the gospel of John, Jesus describes how He is the Good Shepherd. At first the disciples don't understand Him, so He further clarifies His point:

> *Those who heard Jesus use this illustration didn't understand what he meant, so he explained it to them: "I tell you the truth, I am the gate for the sheep. All who came before me were thieves and robbers. But the true sheep did not listen to them.*
> *Yes, I am the gate. Those who come in through me will be saved. They will come and go freely and will find good pastures. The thief's purpose is to steal and kill and destroy. My purpose is to give them a rich and satisfying life."*
>
> —John 10:6–10

The idea of Jesus being our Good Shepherd brings home for us two key ideas as we wrap up our dialogue about emotional trauma and healing.

Our emotional distress has been a thief. The biblical text says, "The thief's purpose is to steal and kill and destroy" (John 10:10). How much sleep has our pain stolen from us? How many opportunities have we lost because we were zoning out rather than tuning in? How many relationships have been ripped apart because we were reacting to past wounds?

Yet Jesus is saying that despite the influence of hardship, which none of us can escape, He is on the scene to usher in life in all of its fullness.

We know that we are thriving when we handle our life challenges much differently than we did when we were in *The Trauma Zone*. It is as if we are on one of those home shows where they do a *before* and *after* shot. Our thriving is the *after* shot, and in it we make a strategic shift from fear to love.

Before we knew how trauma worked, it "worked us over."

The heart of emotional trauma is living in fear and overreacting to most demands. But when we are thriving, we handle our disappointments differently. We learn to overpower our challenges with the love of God that is inside of us. His love fills us with a vision of how our difficulties are being used by Him to strengthen our character and empower us to help others who are suffering from similar pain.

MASTERED TO MASTERY

Before we knew how trauma worked, it "worked us over." We know now that our healing has significantly progressed when we understand how trauma functions. Our trauma used to be a mystery to us. But we've figured it out. The Trauma DJ gives perfectly bad advice, so when we consistently do the opposite of what that inner voice of panic directs us to do, we get much better. We thrive.

OVERWHELMED TO OVERCOMER

And finally, we know that we are thriving when we just get tired of being overwhelmed by our hurts. We experience hurts, but we don't let them have the final word anymore. God's strength inside us has the final word. Isaiah's vision of transformed people crescendos in this passage:

In the last days, the mountain of the Lord's house will
be the highest of all—the most important place on
earth. It will be raised above the other hills,
and people from all over the world
will stream there to worship.

People from many nations will come and say,
"Come, let us go up to the mountain of the Lord,
to the house of Jacob's God. There he will teach us his
ways, and we will walk in his paths."
For the Lord's teaching will go out from Zion;
his word will go out from Jerusalem.

The Lord will mediate between nations and will settle
international disputes. They will hammer their swords
into plowshares and their spears into pruning hooks.
Nation will no longer fight against nation,
nor train for war anymore.

Come, descendants of Jacob,
let us walk in the light of the Lord!

—Isaiah 2:2–5

Our trauma has been a time of war for us. But as we develop the courage to thrive, in the ageless words of the eloquent prophet, all the nations "will hammer their swords into plowshares and their spears into pruning hooks" (Isaiah 2:4). We can do the same thing. We can overcome the turmoil in our lives.

When we thrive, our healing mushrooms. We are not perfect, but who wants that burden? We have something better. Our light can be seen. We are able to make a difference in the world around us. We gratefully enjoy the life God has given us. We relax more. We smile more. We are more confident. We don't allow setbacks to cripple us. We embrace opportunities to grow. We've changed our address from 666 *Trauma Zone Boulevard* to 777 *Transformation Highway.* Amen.

God's strength inside us has the final word.

Self-Help **RESOURCES**

Alcoholics for Christ—An interdenominational, nonprofit, Christian fellowship that ministers to three groups: alcoholics or substance abusers, family members (those who relate regularly with an alcoholic or substance abuser), and adult children (individuals who were raised in alcoholic, substance abuse, or dysfunctional families). http://www.alcoholicsforchrist.com.

Alcoholics Victorious—Support groups that offer a "safe environment where recovering people who recognize Jesus Christ as their 'Higher Power' gather together and share their experience, strength, and hope." http://crc.iugm.org.

Celebrate Recovery—A ministry of Saddleback Valley Community Church. Offers a Bible-based curriculum for support groups and a growing national network of groups. http://www.celebraterecovery.com.

Christians in Recovery—"A group of recovering Christians dedicated to mutual sharing of faith, strength and hope as we live each day in recovery. We work to regain and maintain balance and order in our lives through active discussion of the Bible, and experiences in our own recovery from abuse, family dysfunction, depression, anxiety, grief, relationships and/or addictions of alcohol, drugs, food, pornography, sexual addiction, etc." http://www.christians-in-recovery.com.

Christian Survivors—An active community for survivors of all types of abuse. Their aim is to bring friendship and support to survivors in need and ultimately to help one another come to a place of healing. http://www.christiansurvivors.com.

Confident Kids—A Bible-based support group offering a life skills curriculum that helps families with children ages 4–12 deal with the stresses of living in today's world. http://www.confidentkids.com.

Focus on the Family—Focus has a staff of more than twenty licensed Christian counselors available to talk with you. Call (719) 531-3400 Monday-Friday 9-4:30 (Mountain time), and ask for the Counseling department at extension 7700. One of the counselors' assistants will arrange for a counselor to call you back at no charge to you.

Freedom from Addiction—http://www.freedomfromaddiction.org.

National Association for Christian Recovery—Resources for Christians recovering from addiction, abuse, or trauma. The NACR has no local chapters or groups. They strongly encourage participation in AA and other Twelve-Step programs. http://www.nacronline.com.

Overcomer's Outreach—A network of support groups that use the Bible and the 12 Steps of Alcoholics Anonymous to minister to individuals who are affected by alcohol, mind altering drugs, sexual addiction, gambling, food, and other compulsive behaviors or dependencies. http://www.overcomersoutreach.org.

Pure Intimacy—A ministry of Focus on the Family. Focus on sexual addiction. http://www.pureintimacy.org.

Pure Online—"To enable men and women to conquer sexual issues like pornography addiction and sex addiction and regain control of their lives." http://www.pureonline.com.

RSA Ministries—"A fellowship of men and women who share their experience, strength, and hope for recovery from compulsive sexual behaviors through Christ." http://www.rsaministries.org.

Recommended READING

Anderson, Neil T. *Freedom from Addiction: Breaking the Bondage of Addiction and Finding Freedom in Christ.* Ventura, CA: Gospel Light, 1997.

Arterburn, Stephen. *Every Heart Restored Workbook.* New York: Random House, 2004.

_____. *Healing Is a Choice: Ten Decisions That Will Transform Your Life and Ten Lies That Can Prevent You From Making Them.* Nashville: Thomas Nelson, 2005.

Austin, Sandy. *Angry Teens and the Parents Who Love Them.* Kansas City, MO: Beacon Hill Press, 2002.

Baker, John. *Stepping Out of Denial into God's Grace, Participant's Guide #1, Celebrate Recovery Program.* Grand Rapids, MI: Zondervan, 2005.

Bottke, Allison. *God Allows U-Turns for Teens.* Bloomington, MN: Bethany House Publishers, 2006.

Carder, Dave, Earl Henslin, and John Townsend. *Secrets of Your Family Tree: Healing for Adult Children of Dysfunctional Families.* Chicago: Moody Publishers, 1995.

Cloud, Dr. Henry, and Dr. John Townsend. *God Will Make a Way*. Franklin, TN: Integrity Publishers, 2005.

_____. *What to Do When You Don't Know What to Do: Bad Habits & Addictions*. Franklin, TN: Integrity Publishers, 2005.

Daniels, Robert. *The War Within: Gaining Victory in the Battle for Sexual Purity*. Wheaton, IL: Crossway Books, 2005.

Dayton, Howard. *Free and Clear: God's Roadmap to Debt Free Living*. Chicago: Moody Publishers, 2006.

DeMoss, Nancy Leigh. *Lies Women Believe and the Truth that Sets Them Free*. Chicago: Moody Publishers, 2002.

Dunn, Jerry G., and Bernard Palmer. *God Is for the Alcoholic* (rev. and expanded). Chicago: Moody Publishers, 1986.

Eckman, David. *Sex, Food, and God: Breaking Free from Temptations, Compulsions, and Addictions*. Eugene, OR: Harvest House Publishers, 2006.

George, Denise. *God's Heart, God's Hands: Reaching Out to Hurting Women*. Birmingham: New Hope Publishers, 2004.

Giunta, "Chaplain Ray." *Grief Recovery Workbook*. Franklin, TN: Integrity Publishers, 2002.

Halvorson, Ron, and Valerie Halvorson. *The Twelve Steps— A Spiritual Journey*. Centralia, WA: RPI Publishing, 1988.

Hegstrom, Paul. *Broken Children, Grown-Up Pain: Understanding the Effects of Your Wounded Past*. Kansas City, MO: Beacon Hill Press, 2001.

Heitritter, Lynn, and Jeanette Vought. *Helping Victims of Sexual Abuse* (updated ed.). Bloomington, MN: Bethany House Publishers, 2006.

Jantz, Gregory L., and Ann McMurray. *Healing the Scars of Emotional Abuse* (rev. ed.). Grand Rapids, MI: Baker Books, 2003.

Laaser, Mark R. *Healing the Wounds of Sexual Addiction.* Grand Rapids, MI: Zondervan, 2004.

Lutzer, Erwin W. *Putting Your Past Behind You: Finding Hope for Life's Deepest Hurts* (rev. and expanded). Chicago: Moody Publishers, 1997.

Meyer, Joyce. *Beauty for Ashes* (rev. ed). Brentwood, TN: Warner Faith, 2003.

Meyer, Rick. *Through the Fire: Spiritual Restoration for Adult Victims of Childhood Sexual Abuse.* Minneapolis: Augsburg Fortress, 2005.

Miller, Molly Ann. *My Husband Has a Secret: Finding Healing for the Betrayal of Sexual Addiction.* Kansas City, MO: Beacon Hill Press, 2005.

Murphey, Cecil. *When Someone You Love Abuses Drugs or Alcohol.* Kansas City, MO: Beacon Hill Press, 2004.

Norberg, Tilda. *Ashes Transformed: Healing from Trauma.* Nashville: Upper Room Publications, 2003.

O'Neil, Mike S. *Power to Choose: Twelve Steps to Wholeness.* Nashville: Sonlight Publishing, 1993.

Richardson, Wendy. *When Too Much Isn't Enough: Ending the Destructive Cycle of AD/HD and Addictive Behavior.* Colorado Springs: NavPress, 2005.

Seamands, Stephen A. *Wounds That Heal: Bringing Our Hurts to the Cross.* Downers Grove, IL: InterVarsity Press, 2003.

Smith, Alice. *Beyond the Lie: Finding Freedom from the Past.* Bloomington, MN: Bethany House Publishers, 2006.

Spickard, Anderson Jr., and Barbara Thompson. *Dying for a Drink: What You and Your Family Should Know About Alcoholism.* Nashville: Thomas Nelson, 2005.

Stephens, Steve, and Pam Vredevelt. *The Wounded Woman.* Sisters, OR: Multnomah Publishers, 2006.

Stoop, David. *Forgiving the Unforgivable.* Ventura, CA: Gospel Light, 2005.

Thompson, David, and Gina Eickhoff. *God's Healing for Hurting Families: Biblical Principles for Reconciliation and Recovery.* Indianapolis: Wesleyan Publishing House, 2004.

Tracy, Steven R. *Mending the Soul: Understanding and Healing Abuse.* Grand Rapids, MI: Zondervan, 2005.

Van Stone, Doris, and Erwin Lutzer. *No Place to Cry: The Hurt & Healing of Sexual Abuse.* Chicago: Moody Publishers, 1990.

Wickwire, Jeff. *The Windshield Is Bigger Than the Rearview Mirror: Changing Your Focus from Past to Promise.* Grand Rapids, MI: Baker Books, 2006.

Williams, Don. *12 Steps with Jesus.* Ventura, CA: Gospel Light, 2004.

Wright, H. Norman. *It's Okay to Cry: A Parent's Guide to Helping Children Through the Losses of Life.* New York: Random House, Inc., 2004.

Yoder, Carolyn. *The Little Book of Trauma Healing: When Violence Strikes and Community Security Is Threatened.* New Malden, Surrey, UK: Good Books, 2006.

Guidelines for **CHOOSING** a Support Person

THE SUPPORT PERSON you choose needs to be:

1. Emotionally stable

    a. Lives consistently with his or her own spiritual values

    b. Recovery from his or her own pain is solid

2. Emotionally available

3. Able to listen without being judgmental

4. Trustworthy—someone with whom you feel comfortable

5. Aware of the limits of his or her experience and will refer you to a professional rather than getting in over his head

6. Able to work collaboratively with a pastor or professional counselor if needed

7. Someone who will not exploit your vulnerability in any way

8. Alert to the issue of self-harm and will urge you to seek professional help

Dr. Collins is available for workshops and conferences.
He can be reached at:
thetraumazone@comcast.net

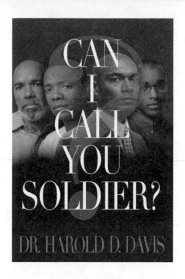

CAN I CALL YOU SOLDIER?
ISBN 0-8024-1166-5
ISBN-13 978-0-8024-1166-2

A generation is under attack...who will protect your family?

The war is at home and the battlefield is in the lives of our young men. In any community, and particularly in the black community, millions of young men feel the void of a role model. For every absent father, complacent leader, and passive bystander, there is someone who will step in and fill the father figure void—whether he is a trustworthy man of God or a dangerous enemy. It's up to us to win this battle and prepare the next generation to join the fight.

"Young men are in desperate need of mentors who model their message. This book challenges the strong among us to become mentors and provides them with the equipment to do so."
    –Rev. William Dwight McKissic, Sr.
    Senior Pastor, Cornerstone Baptist Church

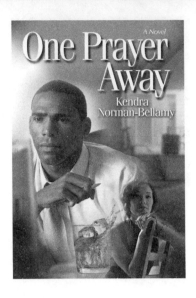

ONE PRAYER AWAY
ISBN 0-8024-6886-1
ISBN-13: 978-0-8024-6886-4

Seven years ago, Mitchell Andrews made the biggest mistake of his life. Now, years later, as he attempts to win back the love of his life and prove that he is a new man, his past begins to creep into his present. He wonders if in his weakest moment God can give him the strength to endure.

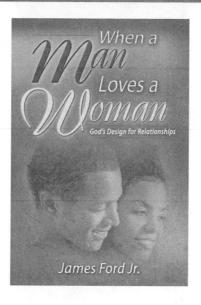

The Negro National Anthem

Lift every voice and sing
Till earth and heaven ring,
Ring with the harmonies of Liberty;
Let our rejoicing rise
High as the listening skies,
Let it resound loud as the rolling sea.
Sing a song full of the faith that the dark past has taught us,
Sing a song full of the hope that the present has brought us,
Facing the rising sun of our new day begun
Let us march on till victory is won.

So begins the Black National Anthem, written by James Weldon Johnson in 1900. Lift Every Voice is the name of the joint imprint of The Institute for Black Family Development and Moody Publishers.

Our vision is to advance the cause of Christ through publishing African-American Christians who educate, edify, and disciple Christians in the church community through quality books written for African Americans.

Since 1988, the Institute for Black Family Development, a 501(c)(3) nonprofit Christian organization, has been providing training and technical assistance for churches and Christian organizations. The Institute for Black Family Development's goal is to become a premier trainer in leadership development, management, and strategic planning for pastors, ministers, volunteers, executives, and key staff members of churches and Christian organizations. To learn more about The Institute for Black Family Development, write us at:

The Institute for Black Family Development
15151 Faust
Detroit, MI 48223

We hope you enjoy this book from Moody Publishers. Our goal is to provide high-quality, thought-provoking books and products that connect truth to your real needs and challenges. For more information on other books and products written and produced from a biblical perspective, go to www.moodypublishers. com or write to:

Moody Publishers/LEV
820 N. LaSalle Boulevard
Chicago, IL 60610
www.moodypublishers.com